What people are saying about …

LUCKY

"Glenn Packiam is a thinker who does not overthink. He is an artist who does not manipulate. He is a pastor who understands that truth is more valuable than spiritual emotionalism. *Lucky* is a prophetic work for today. Glenn beautifully articulates the call in *everyone's* life to carry something extraordinary. This book is a strong answer to the prayers of the kingdom-minded."

Jon Egan, worship leader and songwriter,
Desperation Band and New Life Church

"*Lucky* is one of those books that makes you want to sit back, pause, and rethink your life in light of God's ridiculous love. The message of this book has the potential to reshape the imaginations of a new generation of Christ followers and inspire them to live out the full implications of God's kingdom come in the "here and now." This will be a book that I encourage my entire congregation to read."

Lee Cummings, lead pastor of Radiant
Church in Kalamazoo, MI, and director of
Resurrection Life Churches International

Praise for …

SECONDHAND JESUS

"Digging through the ruins of a 'house built on sand,' Glenn Packiam lays bare the shameless lies of a way of religion, very popular these days in America, without foundations in Jesus or Scripture. But it is far more than exposé. This is an honest, personal, detailed story of a Christian leader refusing cynicism and embracing forgiveness and hope."

Eugene H. Peterson, professor
emeritus of spiritual theology, Regent
College, Vancouver, B.C., Canada

"Glenn Packiam is not only a gifted songwriter and worship leader, penning songs that capture the heart of our generation, but he is also a gifted writer whose textured voice needs to be heard. *Secondhand Jesus* is a much-needed challenge for every believer to embrace knowing God like they never have before."

Margaret Feinberg, popular speaker
and author of *Scouting the Divine*

"Glenn Packiam is an authentic Christ-follower, and as his pastor, I am privileged to watch him teach and lead others on this journey to having a firsthand faith in Jesus. This book is a must-read for anyone wanting more in their walk with Jesus."

Brady Boyd, senior pastor of New Life Church

"What a great read! Page after page I found myself hooked. Glenn has written a book that not only engaged my mind, but also made my heart beat faster for Jesus."

David Nasser, author and speaker

"With clarity and conviction, *Secondhand Jesus* presents the great need to ditch our memorized Christian answers and pursue knowing Jesus for ourselves. Each page is refreshing, challenging, and thought provoking."

David Perkins, director of
Desperation Conferences

"Glenn Packiam offers a personal and thoughtful exploration of the rumors and misconceptions that have plagued the Christian faith. It is a must-read for anyone whose faith has become stale or apathetic, but it also offers something for even the most earnest of believers—a challenge to infuse one's faith with a firsthand relationship with God."

Rob Stennett, author of *The Almost True Story of Ryan Fisher* and *The End Is Now*

LUCKY

LUCKY

HOW THE KINGDOM COMES
TO UNLIKELY PEOPLE

GLENN PACKIAM

David C Cook®

transforming lives together

LUCKY
Published by David C Cook
4050 Lee Vance View
Colorado Springs, CO 80918 U.S.A.

David C Cook Distribution Canada
55 Woodslee Avenue, Paris, Ontario, Canada N3L 3E5

David C Cook U.K., Kingsway Communications
Eastbourne, East Sussex BN23 6NT, England

David C Cook and the graphic circle C logo
are registered trademarks of Cook Communications Ministries.

LCCN 2010942616
ISBN 978-1-4347-6638-0
eISBN 978-1-4347-0364-4

© 2011 Glenn Packiam

The Team: Don Pape, John Blase, Amy Kiechlin,
Sarah Schultz, Caitlyn York, Karen Athen
Cover Design: Rule29

Printed in the United States of America
First Edition 2011

1 2 3 4 5 6 7 8 9 10

123010

To Dad and Mom. I am Lucky to be your son.

CONTENTS

ACKNOWLEDGMENTS

Writing a book can feel like a lonely endeavor. You disappear at odd hours of the day and night and sit quietly with your thoughts, writing, erasing, rewriting. If someone saw me while I was writing—with my eyes glazed as I stare at nothing in particular, my lips moving to form words and my fingers frozen a half inch above the keyboard, waiting to write those words down—they would think I've lost my mind. At times I'm not sure that I haven't! When the phrase is right, I feed the blinking cursor more letters. When I'm stuck, that thin black line taunts me as it pulses and I contemplate getting a snack or a drink or both. Then, when a chapter is "done," I have to resist the urge to send it to all of my friends, begging their feedback.

But writing never truly happens alone. I am in the company of all the writers I have read. Their thoughts bounce in my head, from the back to the forefront of my mind. And then there are the many conversations. How many unsuspecting friends, upon hearing that I was writing another book, innocently asked what it was about only to find themselves taken hostage as I launched into a twenty-minute exposition of each chapter.

Thankfully, I have been surrounded by amazing people who gladly interacted with me about this book, both in written form and in conversation. You have all helped make my thoughts clearer, my writing crisper, and this book better than it would have been had I truly been alone in writing it.

Here are a few specific people that I feel *lucky* to have in my life:

To Don Pape, for your endless encouragement. You and Ruth are a source of strength to Holly and me.

To John Blase for your ever-thoughtful approach to this book, for your probing questions and challenges to make sections of it stronger.

To Eugene Peterson, for inspiring the thought of using "lucky" in the Beatitudes, for the gift of a visit in your home, for the honor of your words in the foreword. You are a picture of pastoral grace and faithfulness.

To Brady Boyd, for your humble and gracious leadership. You have helped me flourish in this place where I have been planted. You are gift to our church and to me.

To my friends Aaron Stern, Patton Dodd, Jeremiah Parks, Jon Egan, and many others, who endured many sermonizing moments in our ever-rich friendships as I was wrestling with this content.

To my wife, Holly, for allowing me the time late at night to go into my study and sit behind a glowing screen for hours on end as I tried to turn thoughts into words. You let me talk over and over with you about the themes of this book, and you helped me find the places where the ideas may matter most. I am lucky to be loved by you.

To my children, Sophia, Norah, and Jonas, for reminding me what to be thankful for each day and for helping me keep my laptop closed on the weekends—though I haven't always done it well.

To you. To the reader holding this book. Thank you. Thank you for taking the time to read. Thank you for choosing to explore this idea, this theme. Thank you for spending a few hours with me. I pray the Holy Spirit quickens your mind, awakens your heart, and emboldens your actions. May the kingdom that has come to you go through to others.

FOREWORD
by Eugene Peterson

I have just finished reading the book you are holding in your hands—Glenn Packiam's *Lucky*. And I'm feeling lucky. I'm feeling lucky to have spent a few hours in the company of a pastor who cares enough about the gospel of Jesus and the kingdom of God to take them seriously on their own terms, to respect their integrity. He doesn't adapt them to the American consumer culture. He doesn't strain to make them relevant to a secularized way of life that is only interested in God on its own terms. He is not a Bible salesman selling a religious product at cut-rate prices.

He begins by throwing us into the deep end of the pool, introducing the centerpiece of Christian teaching with Jesus blessing a quartet of losers: the poor, the hungry, the grief-stricken, the despised (Luke 6:20–23). And the water is freezing cold. But Pastor Packiam doesn't apologize—he seems to think that Jesus means what He says. I hear him saying to us, "Get used to it."

And we do get used to it, largely because the biblical message is conveyed to us on its own terms, as narrative. Not "truths" or "principles" or "advice," proof texts proving that Jesus didn't really mean what He said. The story, from Genesis to Jesus, gathers us into relationships and plot. Nothing impersonal here.

Not only do the Scriptures retain their original "storied," relational character in the pages you are about to read, but the poor, hungry, grief-stricken, and despised also retain theirs. None of them are lumped into categories and accounted for by statistics. They have personal names; they live in locatable places. We find ourselves in the company of a pastor who knows the men, women, and children he serves in Jesus' name. The stories convey a sense of accuracy and dignity. I don't catch a hint of sentimentalism or propagandistic manipulation in the telling. These are not poster-child renditions to manipulate our emotions.

There is also this: The poor, grief-stricken, and despised, that by now we are becoming accustomed to recognizing as lucky, make their appearance in Malaysia, Portland, Chicago, Starbucks, Cambodia, Detroit, Colorado Springs, and Uganda. Lest we stereotype the luckless as people we will never see, or maybe the person we look at in the mirror every morning, we are brought into a multicultural, world-embracing community in which God is doing His kingdom work.

This *is* explicitly kingdom work, kingdom-of-God work, a kingdom already here but also in the making. We are not just picking up the pieces in the wake of the expulsion from Eden and the confusion at Babel. God is making a kingdom, and Christ is King. We are part of the work being done and also participants in the work. As we participate, we realize that we bring no qualifications to the task, none at all. Lest we get in the way of the kingdom work that God is doing, Jesus redefines us all as the poor, the hungry, the grief-stricken, and the despised. Then as Pastor Packiam deftly and clearly works us and others into the kingdom story, we realize how thoroughly blessed we are—*lucky,* lucky indeed.

Eugene H. Peterson
Professor Emeritus of Spiritual Theology at Regent College
Vancouver, British Columbia

CHAPTER ONE

FEELING LUCKY?

Bud had had a run of bad luck. When he was eight years old, his mother died. His father, unable or unwilling to raise him, later sent Bud to an orphanage. When he got out, he struggled to adapt to society and earn a decent living. He spent most of his adult life puttering on different jobs, from spray painting pipelines to being a cook and truck driver for circuses and carnivals. He had never owned a home or a car. Money had been hard to come by. Things had gotten so bad that he had even served a twenty-eight-day jail sentence for writing too many bad checks.

Then one day, Bud decided to buy a lottery ticket. At the time, he was on disability and had a grand total of $2.46 in his bank account. He had nothing to lose and over sixteen million dollars to win.

It happened. William "Bud" Post III won $16.2 million dollars in the Pennsylvania lottery in 1988. Luck, it seemed, was smiling on him.[1]

———

Who do you think is lucky? Who, in your estimation, has it made?

Is it the person with lots of money and Hollywood good looks? Is it the one who spends afternoons on the golf course or at the five-star health spa? Maybe it's the one with the perfect job and ideal marriage and dutiful children who make the von Trapps look like vagabonds. *Whoever it is*, you may say, *it's not me.*

When we think of a lucky person, we think of someone like Bud Post, an average guy who grew up like we did, with challenges and adversity, who somehow happened to buy the winning lottery ticket. There's just enough about *them* that makes you believe they are just like you. They may have had modest talent, sure, and a solid work ethic, yes. But they had a few big breaks you didn't have. They got *lucky*. They were born into the right family, at the right time, in the right city. They grew up with the right connections and were given the right opportunities. And *that's* how they got where they are.

We're not far off. We were this close, you say. *But then …* The divorce. The kid who got your son to try that drug that left him addicted. The cancer that came like a thief in the night and stole your wife's health and vandalized your finances. The downturn in the economy that turned into a recession. The investment you leveraged everything to make that was just a few months too late. The bubble that burst and left you mired in debt instead of swimming in wealth. You're Bud Post pre-1988, with a losing lottery ticket and no stunning reversal of fortunes.

Successful people, people who have made something of their lives, usually try to deflect any association with luck. Gary Player, the South African golfer who won nine Majors, famously shrugged off an accusation of being lucky on the golf course by saying, "Well, the more I practice, the luckier I get." People on the outside looking in believe in luck—because they are sure that's all that separates them from the successful and because they hope that their fortunes will one day be reversed. People on the inside prefer to credit talent and hard work.

Malcolm Gladwell is known for offering a paradigm-shattering, contrarian view of social trends and behavioral norms we take for granted. In his book *Outliers*, Gladwell tackles the subject of the extraordinarily successful. The conventional view is that, if you add talent to hard work, you'll get a fairly predictable outcome: success. And because this is true for the moderately successful, we assume it's also true for the outrageously successful—the outliers like professional athletes or world-renowned violinists or Bill Gates.

Gladwell, however, demonstrates that, while all outliers have a base of talent and a history of hard work, that's only enough to get them to a certain point. What pushes them over the edge are things we may not have thought to consider, like date of birth, country of birth, access to education or technology, a family with disposable income to afford road trips and other creative-learning environments. His book is stocked with stories that make the point. Talent and hard work may get you some success, but to be an outlier, to be extraordinarily successful, you also need a little luck.

Gladwell's theory only reinforces what we've always suspected deep down: Others have it made, but not me. A deep divide runs between the glamorous, wealthy, successful people out there and the ordinary, average, unspectacular you and me. We're always on the outside looking in. And those others, well, they may not admit it, but they're just plain *lucky*.

They bought the winning lottery ticket.

If only we could be so lucky.

———

But that sort of luck isn't what it seems.

Bud Post chose to get his winnings in twenty-six annual payments of roughly half a million dollars. Within two weeks of collecting his first installment, he had spent over three hundred thousand of it. Three months later, he was half a million dollars in debt—thanks to, among other things, a restaurant in Florida he had leased for his sister and brother, a used-car lot complete with a fleet of cars he had bought for another brother, and a twin-engine plane he had bought for himself even though he didn't have a pilot's license.

A year later, debt wasn't his only problem. He became estranged from his siblings, and a county court ordered him to stay away from his sixth wife after he allegedly fired a rifle at her vehicle. Bud Post was Dale Carnegie in reverse: a millionaire losing friends and alienating people while accruing a mountain of debt. When his former landlady sued him for a portion of the winnings to pay off old debts, Bud was finished. The judge ruled that she was entitled to a third of his lottery winnings, and when Bud couldn't pay it, the judge ordered that all further payments of his winnings be frozen until the dispute was resolved.

Desperate for cash, Bud sold his Pennsylvania mansion in 1996 for a miserable sixty-five thousand dollars and auctioned off the remaining payments of his winnings. With a little over two and a half million dollars remaining, Bud hoped that people would finally leave him alone. But the person who created the most trouble was the one he could never escape: himself. He squandered it on two homes, a truck, three cars, two Harleys, a couple of big-screen TVs, a boat, a camper, and a few computers. By 1998, ten years after winning $16.2 million dollars, Bud Post was once again living on disability payments.

"I was much happier when I was broke," he lamented.

William "Bud" Post III died at age sixty-six of a respiratory failure, broke and alone.

An Unexpected Word

We think of luck as simply a positive reversal of fortune or chance occurrence that worked out in our favor. Like winning the lottery. Jesus sees it as far more. He knows it takes more than changing your conditions and surroundings to make you lucky. It takes more than money or comfort or success. It takes the arrival of the kingdom of God. And that is no chance occurrence.

When Jesus raised His eyes to address the crowd that had gathered that day, He must have seen some interesting people. These were not the important big-city types. Those would come later when Paul joined the team and traveled to various cities. No, these first followers were country folks. Simple, well-meaning, kindhearted peasants. Luke, the gospel writer, doesn't mention a name we might know or even a grouping—like Pharisee or Sadducee or scribe or lawyer—we might recognize other than "the disciples." This is simply a crowd. A crowd of ordinary, unspectacular people. Sure, the twelve He had chosen were there, but they may not have looked like the most promising bunch either.

So when Jesus began to speak, it's important to remember who He was looking at. He wasn't sermonizing, delivering a prepared oratory masterpiece to a mass generic audience. It wasn't a canned speech He had taken on the circuit. Jesus, full of compassion, sat on the plain and spoke. To *them.* To the unlucky, to the outcast and insignificant, to the overlooked and undervalued.

To *them.*

And He began with this word: "Blessed."

Except it wasn't quite that word.

Both Luke and Matthew chose the Greek word *makarios* to capture our Lord's opening word in the Beatitudes.[2] *Makarios* simply means "fortunate, happy." In secular Greek literature, it is used to describe the blissful state of the gods. It is not an inherently religious word.[3] The Greek word more like our words "blessed" or "blessing" is *eulogia. Eulogia* is often used to invite or invoke God's blessing and also to bless God. That word was, of course, available to Jesus—and Luke and Matthew. But He—they—chose *makarios* instead.

In the Septuagint, the Greek translation of the Hebrew Old Testament—the version of the Scriptures many in Jesus' day would have used—*makarios* is the word used most often to translate the Hebrew word *asar.* But *asar* is not the word for a "God-blessed" person or thing or action. In fact it is rarely used of God blessing anything or anyone.[4] *Asar* is simply "happy, favored, prosperous" and has the connotation of one whose paths are straight, which is a way of saying someone for whom things always unfold neatly and nicely.

The psalmist in Psalm 1 uses *asar* to say, "*Blessed* is the man who does not walk in the counsel of the wicked or stand in the way of sinners or sit in the seat of mockers." It's also the word the queen of Sheba used when she exclaimed, "How happy your men must be!" as a way of praising Solomon (1 Kings 10:8). Even though *asar* has the implication, by the context of its use, that God is the true source or reason for the person's blessedness, it is not inherently a religious word. It's a marketplace word, used to simply say that a person is fortunate, that he "has it good."

If we were to use a word today for *makarios*, we would choose the word *lucky*. Not *lucky* as in the result of randomness. Not *lucky* as in the reward for properly acknowledging a superstition or a charm. It is neither the product of erratic chance nor the result of currying favor with some capricious god. It is simply *lucky* as we use it conversationally: *You lucky dog, you get to take a vacation next week! Or, Lucky you! You just got a promotion in the middle of a recession! Makarios,* as one New Testament commentator suggested, is akin to the Aussie slang, "Good on ya, mate," which is rather like the American, "Good for you!" Which are both like saying, "Lucky you!"

The irony of this word choice is heightened when we imagine Jesus looking at these ordinary, unspectacular people and exclaiming, "Lucky you!" He might as well have said, "Lucky are the unlucky!"[5]

> *Lucky are you who are poor,*
> *for yours is the kingdom of God.*

Lucky are you who hunger now,
*   for you will be satisfied.*
Lucky are you who weep now,
*   for you will laugh.*
Lucky are you when men hate you,
*   when they exclude you and insult you*
*   and reject your name as evil, because of the Son of*
*   Man.*[6]

Why would Jesus say that? Why would He call these unlikely and unlucky people, *lucky?*

An Unlikely People

The Jews of Jesus' day knew that they were the lucky ones. They were Abraham's descendants. They were the insiders. They were God's special covenant people.

Abraham's family had been chosen to be God's people—by grace! And because it was Abraham's descendants who were enslaved in Egypt, God heard the cries of *His* people and sent Moses to rescue them—again, by grace! Then, after they had been chosen as God's people, after they had been saved from Egypt, Moses gave them the law.

The law was not how they became the covenant people of God; the law was how they were to live as the covenant people of God. For the Jews of the first century, the Mosaic law itself was not seen as a means of *becoming* God's people; rather it was a sort of badge of honor displaying that they *were indeed* God's people. You might say that the law was a sign of their luckiness. And yet the law was also a clear reminder of how far they had fallen short. They were well aware of their transgressions against the law. Even worse, their history was stained by their covenant unfaithfulness. Still God's steady faithfulness to Israel remained. And because of that, hope that Israel would be "lucky" again—that they would be delivered from their enemies, be freed from exile, and have their calling fulfilled—was alive in their hearts.

All that history and drama of privilege and failure and faithfulness and hope and expectation are the backdrop for Jesus' most famous sermon, the Sermon on the Mount found in Matthew 5—7 and the condensed but parallel Sermon on the Plain in Luke 6. The Sermon consists of quite possibly the most written-about passages of Scripture in church history.

One of the most common views is to see the Sermon as a new law. There are indeed striking parallels between the story of Moses and the story of Jesus. Moses came out of Egypt, went through the waters of the Red Sea and the wilderness on Sinai, and ascended the mountain and came down with the law; Jesus came out of Egypt (as a child), went through the waters of baptism and the wilderness of temptation, and ascended the hill[7] to deliver this sermon. Matthew's phrase "He opened His mouth and began to teach them" (5:2 NASB) is not filler. It's a Hebrew idiom to denote one who speaks with divine authority, one who utters the very oracles of God. The view of the Sermon as a new kind of law can help us see something that was likely part of Jesus' point: He means to say, to those who thought they were so good at keeping Moses' law, that unless they kept it even in their hearts they would not enter the kingdom. This is certainly clear in Matthew 5:20 when He says, "Unless your righteousness surpasses that of the Pharisees and the teachers of the law, you will certainly not enter the kingdom of heaven." In the later sections of the Sermon on the Mount, when Jesus says, "You have heard … but I say unto you …," it becomes clear that Jesus meant for them to internalize the law of Moses. The truth is, the law was always meant to be internalized, written on their hearts, and obeyed out of love for God and neighbor. Moses had said as much in his day, and later the prophets revisited the theme. Jesus, revealing the Father's intent, was giving the final word. It's not enough not to murder; you cannot hate. It's not enough not to commit adultery; you cannot lust. And so on. For the first listeners, the Sermon would have led them to realize the futility of their efforts and to respond with some version of the question "Who can live like this?" And that would have been exactly the thing Jesus was after—to show that no one could truly fulfill the law alone.

This is where some of our modern teachers have made the mistake of throwing the whole thing out. "It's all there just to frustrate us, to lead us to a Savior who will forgive and redeem us," they say. But that is only half true. Jesus does mean for us to live in the way He describes in His Sermon: He wants us to be righteous from the inside out. In fact, if we draw a parallel between when and why the Mosaic law was given and this so-called "new law" of Christ, the point becomes clearer. Just as the Mosaic law was given to a people who had already been chosen by grace and saved by grace, so for those who are in Christ, this new, inside-out way of living is for those who have already become God's people by grace. It would be impossible to treat it as simply good moral advice and discouraging to attempt to obey it as a means of "getting in." Jesus meant for His Sermon to be viewed as the way to *live* as the people of God, not the way to *become* the people of God. The great teachers throughout church history, from Chrysostom and Augustine in the fourth and fifth centuries to Luther and the Reformers in the sixteenth century, understood that the entire Sermon must be read from the perspective of one who has already been saved by grace through faith. Martin Luther said, "Christ is saying nothing in this sermon about how we become Christians, but only about the works and fruit that no one can do unless he already is a Christian and in a state of grace."[8]

Because we are in Christ, we are now the covenant people of God regardless of our ethnicity and national identity. We are "in"— by grace! We are rescued—by grace! Feeling lucky? *But wait.* There's more. We have received the Holy Spirit, which means that living this way—this way of inward righteousness—is not merely up to our own strength. We don't simply say, "Thanks, God. I'll take it from here." It is God's design that, once we are saved through Him, we receive the power, through His Spirit, to actually become the kind of person He is describing.

The Sermon, far from being a list of conditions for entry in the kingdom, is an elaborate description of how this new people of God, empowered by grace through the Holy Spirit, are to now live. Not only have we—outsiders and onlookers—been brought into the kingdom because of Jesus; now, *because* we are in the kingdom, because we are living under God's rule, this is the kind of life that God the Spirit produces in us.

Feeling lucky, yet?

Unexpected Outcomes

This is all well and good for the bulk of the Sermon on the Mount and the Sermon on the Plain, but what about the first few verses of each, the Beatitudes? Some have suggested that the Beatitudes are a "ladder of virtue," an ascending list of qualities to be attained, a sort of growth chart for the Christian. But that would make persecution the final stage in our maturation, an idea that would have made perfect sense in one era and none in another. And it would create a sort of hierarchy, distinguishing between the "serious" followers of Christ who obey the full list and the "casual Christians" who choose not to.

Others have said it is a pronouncement of the way things are, an unveiling of the mystery of life. But this would be odd, for we know that not all who mourn are comforted. And the daily news is proof that the meek never inherit much of anything.

Many teachers have taken a more moderate path, shying away from calling them a ladder of virtue or a pronouncement of the way things are and seeing them, instead, as prescriptions on how to live. Should we pursue poverty and sorrow and persecution? To read the Beatitudes as blessings that are being given because of something these people have done requires a sort of spiritualizing of the text. We would have to take being "poor in spirit" as a way of saying "morally bankrupt" and make "mourning" synonymous with "repentance." We would emphasize that to "hunger and thirst for righteousness" is to desire and long for the kind of inward "rightness of being" that only God can give us in Christ. This sort of reading of the Beatitudes has been emphasized through the centuries, from Augustine in the fourth century to the esteemed Dr. Martyn-Lloyd Jones in the twentieth century, and with good reason. It is hard to miss the progression from admitting our state of spiritual poverty to mourning in repentance to beginning to crave for an inward righteousness, and so on. Reading the Beatitudes as blessings on certain spiritual virtues would certainly be consistent with what the Scriptures teach us about growing in Christ.

But the bulk of writing and teaching on the Beatitudes has zeroed in on Matthew's list rather than Luke's. Luke's list is half the size of Matthew's (four instead of eight) and leaves no room for reading it as a list of spiritual virtues. Luke simply has Jesus announcing blessing on those who are "poor," not those who are "poor in spirit"; those who "hunger now," not those who "hunger and thirst for righteousness"; those who "weep now," and who are hated, excluded, and insulted. Luke's rendering is terse and dry. They resist spiritualization and require another way of hearing them—not a way that is in conflict with the much-written-about way, and not a way that was altogether absent in the historical expositions, just one that is not as heavily stressed. Often overshadowed by Matthew's spiritual "Blesseds," Luke's shorter, sparser Beatitudes suggest another lens for Jesus' words:

What if Jesus was announcing blessing on these people not *because* of their state but *in spite* of it?

Could it be that Jesus is not saying, "Blessed are you *because* you are poor," but rather, "Blessed are you *in spite* of being poor, for the kingdom has come to even such as you"? Reading it this way begins to make more sense. In this light, those who are mourning are now blessed because they will—in God's kingdom that Jesus is bringing—be comforted. They are not considered lucky because of their mourning; they are lucky because they are receiving—and will receive in fullness—the unexpected good fortune of God's comfort in spite of their mourning now. The focus of the blessing—especially in Luke's gospel—is on the latter portion of each Beatitude, not on the opening phrase. Luck is not in their initial conditions—of poverty and hunger and mourning and persecution—but rather in their unexpected outcomes: The kingdom of heaven in its fullness, comfort, and reward is theirs.

Dietrich Bonhoeffer, the German theologian who paid a great price for living out his convictions and opposing an immoral military regime in World War II, wrote a landmark book called *The Cost of Discipleship*. Experiencing the high cost of following Jesus and His teachings in his own life, Bonhoeffer has us read these words of blessing in the shadow of the cross. Referring to Luke 6, he wrote:

> Therefore Jesus calls His disciples blessed. He spoke to men who had already responded to the power of his call, and it is that call that made them poor, afflicted and hungry. He calls them blessed, not because of their privation, or the renunciation they have made, for these are not blessed themselves. Only the call and the promise ... can justify the beatitudes.[9]

Only the call and the promise can justify the beatitudes. Not their condition but Christ's call; not their poverty but God's promise. Perhaps Bonhoeffer was echoing his German theological forefather Martin Luther, who also would not narrow his reading of the Beatitudes as merely a list of virtues. In Luther's lectures on the

Sermon on the Mount, he pointed out that the people—even the crowd in Matthew's gospel and not only the disciples in Luke's—are not being praised for being poor or for mourning. Those are not virtues in and of themselves. They are being called blessed because the kingdom of God has come *even to such as these.*

The Beatitudes are chiefly an announcement, a proclamation that now, because of Jesus, everything will be different. Indeed it is already becoming different. If we can use our modern conversational expressions, we might sum up Jesus' message like this: "Lucky you, for the kingdom of God has come to the unlikely and the unlucky."

And yet.

There *is* something about being the unlikely and unlucky, the marginalized and the overlooked, that sets us up perfectly to receive what God is offering. By paying attention to what that is, we can gain the right posture of heart even if our earthly circumstances are grand and prosperous. It does, to an extent, like the rest of the Sermon (whether in Matthew or Luke), paint a picture of the type of person we become when the kingdom comes to us, the type of life God's reign will produce in us. That is how we make sense of the blessing in Matthew's Beatitudes on the pure in heart or the peacemakers.

To keep this book within my scope, I will not attempt to add to the already rich and historic writing on Matthew's Sermon on the Mount. Instead I will constrain our conversations to the four Beatitudes found in Luke's gospel. This will help our focus to be on how the unlikely have become lucky because of what Jesus has done and is doing in us. As we talk, in the chapters that follow, about each of the four Beatitudes in Luke 6, we will unpack two dimensions: how these particular people are lucky *in spite* of their conditions, and how their precise conditions *prepare* them to surrender to God's reign. Woven through our conversation will also be a recovery of the call that comes with the blessing: Since we've become the lucky ones, we must become carriers of this blessing to others who are unlikely and unlucky in our day.

For now it is enough to see that these people, the unlikely and the unlucky, are suddenly lifted to the level of admiration—*how happy for you!*—because the kingdom of God has come to them. This is Christ's announcement: The kingdom has come to unlikely, unexpected people. And for that, they are lucky indeed. Lucky with a capital L.

The Message

When Eugene Peterson, known now as the translator of the well-known and well-loved *The Message* Bible, pastored in the Baltimore area, there was a woman who came in a bit late, sat at the back, and sneaked out before the service was over. She had never been to church before. She was in her forties, and she dressed like a hippie whose time had past, but the joy on her face was new. Her husband was an alcoholic, her son a drug addict, and her friends relentless in persuading her to come to church. Week after week, she repeated this pattern of being fashionably late in arriving and serendipitously early in leaving.

Then Peterson taught a series on the life of David. One week in the midst of it, she decided to stay. The benediction was spoken, and there she was, still in her seat. When Peterson stood at the doors to greet people on their way out, she came to him with a look of astonishment. "Pastor, thank you. I've never heard that story before. I just feel so lucky," she said. Week after week, this became her new tradition: to greet the pastor on her way out and say, surprised by the hope, the forgiveness, the redemption she had learned were hers, "I feel so lucky."

It was that experience that made Peterson want to use the word *lucky* as the opening word of each Beatitude in his new translation. But he was not particularly well-known then, and the publishers were already taking an enormous risk allowing for such a modern colloquial translation. The editors got nervous and suggested he stick to the conventional word *blessed* even though the Greek *makarios*, as I've already noted and as Peterson insists, is not a "religious" word. It is a street-language word, not one reserved for hymns and prayers and blessings from God.

Either new editors came along or Peterson earned a little more latitude. When *The Message* translation of the Old Testament Wisdom Books (Job, Psalms, Proverbs, Ecclesiastes, and Song of Songs) rolled out five years later, the word *lucky* showed up eight times. Then the rest of the Old Testament was finished, and it showed up eleven more times.

No passage to me is more beautiful than this:

> *I dare to believe that the luckless will get lucky someday*
> *in you. (Ps. 10:14 MSG)*

Lucky You

If Jesus were sitting across the table from you and said to you that you are blessed, that He counts you as lucky, what would you think?

That's crazy. No, I'm not, you would insist. *I'm ordinary, unspectacular. And besides, I'm too messed up; I've made too many mistakes. I'm the person on the fringes, the margins, the outskirts. I'm not admired or applauded, respected or rewarded. I'm just ... me. And whatever that is, it's not* lucky.

Or you would be tempted to think—as so many TV preachers do—that what this means is that everything you touch will turn to gold. You are blessed, and from here on out, everything is going to work out right. You'll never get sick, never be broke, never be troubled again. You'll live a charmed life. Things are going to get better and better until you fly away to glory. *That's* what it means to be lucky.

Both responses would be wrong.

Jesus took an inherently nonreligious word, a word from normal everyday conversations, and filled it with divine implications. It turns out the ones we ought to call lucky are the ones God is blessing with the arrival of His kingdom. In doing this, Jesus redefined who the lucky ones are. They are not the ones culture lauds as successful, not the ones we secretly aspire to be. He turned our appraisal of the good life on its head. There is a great reversal coming; indeed it has already begun. And the ones who are receiving and participating in the kingdom of God are the ones who are truly lucky, deeply blessed.

Just like the people Jesus addressed, you are called lucky not *because* of your poverty or your hunger or your mourning or the persecution you're enduring. You are lucky because *in spite* of it, you have been invited into the kingdom. It may not mean that your circumstances will immediately change. Many who heard Jesus' words didn't go off and all of a sudden "discover their purpose" and become influential world changers. Many, if not most, of them kept farming. And fishing. And raising their kids and going about their lives.

And yet everything had changed. They had seen a glimpse of God at work. Their hope was now rooted in the belief that Messiah had come. All that was wrong was beginning to be undone.

So it is for you. God has come to you in the midst of your mess and mistakes. He is announcing His arrival into your ordinary unspectacular life and inviting you to follow, to surrender, to live in a different way. God is rescuing and redeeming the world, and you—unlikely you!—have somehow gotten in on it. The trajectory of your life has been altered. You now have a part in the future that God is bringing. Like Abraham, you have been blessed to carry blessing, to live as a luck-bearer to the unlikely and the unlucky. You are receiving and participating in the kingdom of God.

And for that *you* are lucky. So lucky!

DISCUSSION QUESTIONS

1. Who do you consider to be lucky? Who is living a charmed life? Why do you think that?

2. How does this chapter reshape your picture of the person who is to be admired?

3. How is this exposition of Luke's Beatitudes different from the way you've read it in the past?

4. In what ways are you Lucky with a capital *L?*

CHAPTER TWO

LUCK'S BEGINNER

Her eyes spoke before she did. "It was really sad," my wife said to me when I saw her after the service. A young Malaysian Chinese man had driven her to the church, and she had just heard a bit of his story.

We were in Malaysia because I had been invited to speak at a conference there, and we had jumped at the chance to take our kids to see my parents and the country where I had grown up. After nearly thirty hours of traveling—undoubtedly the longest possible route, chosen so we could use frequent-flier miles for two of the tickets—we were there. On the first day of the conference, we felt an immediate connection with the people of the host church. They were kindred hearts. By Sunday morning, after three rich days of ministry and meals and conversations, we had really grown close to these people. So when this young man picked Holly up from the hotel, he felt willing to share his story.

He had moved to the States to go to college through a "twinning program"—an increasingly popular system that allows Malaysian students to do a few years of college in Malaysia and then complete their studies in the United States, Australia, or the UK. While they enjoy their time abroad, many Malaysian students conclude that, because of strong family ties and cultural familiarity, there is simply no place like home. For this young man, things were a bit different. It wasn't that he didn't miss his family or the country that he had grown up in. It was just that he was beginning to really make friends and feel comfortable in western Michigan—as strange as that sounds for someone who grew up near the equator. He liked being in America.

"You know," he said to my wife, "I could have been like Glenn. I really liked being in the States. I wanted to stay on."

Those words for him were free of jealousy and full of regret. He had wanted the life that I have. He had had every intention of continuing to live in the States, yet here he was, back in Malaysia. It wasn't bad. He had secured a good job, having leveraged his degree from an American university. He was involved in his church and surrounded by good friends. No, it wasn't bad at all; it just wasn't the life he had envisioned when he came to America as a college student. And seeing me only reminded him of what could have been, the *if-only*.

After earning his degree, he had applied for a work visa but had been denied because it was the spring of 2002. Only a few months earlier, the devastating terrorist attacks from four hijacked planes had splintered the sense of American peace and stability. New security measures, from airport screening to tightening visa restrictions, were being added daily. Or so it seemed. Patriotism, vigilance, and racial profiling were mixed together in a toxic stew, boiling over on the flames of national fear. A student from a Muslim country wasn't going to get a visa; it didn't matter that Malaysia is a multi-ethnic, multi-religious, democratic Muslim country, or that this particular student was a well-behaved Christ-following Chinese young man. Timing may not be everything, but sometimes it nearly is. He was asking for a visa at the worst possible time.

When I graduated in 1999, I applied for a work visa, and though the process was rigorous, I had no problems whatsoever.

My heart sank as my wife relayed his story to me. A few years later and who knows how things would have turned out. How did I get so lucky?

For that matter, why is anybody lucky? Again, not in the random, win-the-lottery sense of the word, but in the "good for you" sort of way when things just work out right. To be sure, sometimes it may be coincidence, the function of being at the right place at the right time and so on. But if some things aren't random, if some things truly are the results of divine providence, then to what end? If we are, in our more familiar word, *blessed,* then why have we been *blessed?*

Knowing the source of your luck will help determine the reason for it.

Unexpected Expectations

Even Charles Dickens knew as much. In his classic novel set in the mid-nineteenth century, Dickens tells us Pip's story of *Great Expectations* in the first person so we feel what Pip felt and see the world through his eyes. An orphan being raised by his sister, who was twenty years older, and her husband, Pip was a sort of precursor to Huck Finn—a poor, uneducated yet cunning and resourceful boy.

In their meager home not far from the graveyard where Pip's parents were buried, a single slice of bread with butter was a daily delight. And despite the short temper of his sister, the simplemindedness of her husband, and their considerable lack, Pip had a deep affection for them. They were the only father and mother he'd ever known, the only home he'd had.

All of that began to change when Pip was introduced to the extraordinarily wealthy and equally enigmatic Miss Havisham. Miss Havisham's daughter, Estella, it seemed, needed a friend. If Miss Havisham was strange with her aged-yellow wedding dress and dark house and uneaten wedding cake, then Estella was hauntingly beautiful with her fair skin and brown hair. But Estella had been raised to be coldhearted with her beauty, to draw a person in and then push them away. Pip couldn't help but fall for Estella, which made her contempt of him sorely humiliating. Miss Havisham kept requesting Pip's visits and eventually paid for Pip to apprentice his brother-in-law, Joe, as a metalsmith.

So when, about a hundred and thirty pages into the story, Pip learned that he was to be removed from his poor surroundings immediately, moved to the city, and raised as a gentlemen, as a young man who had great expectations, Pip immediately assumed that his fortune had come from Miss Havisham—that her plan was for him to marry Estella, and that his upcoming education and training as a gentleman were in preparation for it. "My dream," Pip thought to himself, "was out; my wild fancy was being surpassed by a sober reality; Miss Havisham was going to make my fortune on a grand scale."[1]

But there was one very big caveat that came with his fortune: He could not know who his benefactor was. To Pip, that just seemed part of Miss Havisham's strange ways. Pip moved to London, engaged in his education, acquired a certain swagger and a mountain of debt to go with it. *Not to worry,* he thought. *I am to come into great wealth. I am a man with great expectations.*

As it turns out—*spoiler alert!*—Pip's fortunes weren't from Miss Havisham. His benefactor was a grizzled convict, the same convict who jumped him in the graveyard by his home in the opening pages of the story. The horror of this revelation unfolded as Pip had to face the miserable way he abandoned Joe, the emptiness of his own hope, and the undesirable predicament of being beholden to an escaped convict.

What Dickens teaches us in this timeless tale is that it is not enough to have great expectations; you must know why you have them and from whence they have come. Knowing the source of your good fortune helps you know how you should live with it. Who the blessing is from will explain why it has come and what you are to do with it.

So. We are to be counted *lucky.* Jesus Himself says so. And our luck is far more than work visas and a wealthy inheritance. Our luck is that the kingdom of God has come to us—yes, even to such as us! But why have we come into this good fortune? Why would God bring His kingdom to us, to the unlikely and the unlucky? Understanding this is the key to ensuring that we don't squander our wealth of blessing on self-absorbed pleasure. We are not blessed for our own sake.

Then why has this luck come? When God made the first humans, why did He bless them? When He called Abraham and his family and set them apart from all other families, what was His goal? Who is the Originator, the Author of Blessing? Who is, in a manner of speaking, *Luck's* Beginner?

To answer that, we must start at the very beginning.

O Adam, Where Art Thou?

In the beginning, God. God made the world, and He called it good. This is how the Jewish-Christian story begins. Man and woman were made to be God's image-bearers, the ones who would rule over creation and care for it in God's name as God would, the ones who would most fully reflect Him. They were to multiply, producing other image-bearers who would reflect and reveal God, and in doing so would cover the earth with His glory.

But the image-bearers were not content to be with God; they wanted to be like Him. More than bearing His image, they wanted His power, His autonomy, His unbound freedom. For the creature to seek freedom from the Creator, to desire to *be* the Creator, is to say, "I don't need You. I can do better without You." It is an affront to the Creator, the ultimate insult. This rebellion was the beginning of evil in the creature and the end of perfectly bearing the image of the Creator. From that moment on, the image was marred, stained, tainted by the rebellion.

The Jewish-Christian story of humanity's origin is the one that seems to best take into account the human capacity for both goodness and noble action—it is the image of God in us!—and the inherent selfishness, twistedness that resides in the basement of our souls. It tells us that we are good creations of a good God and that we are fallen. We are a good creation ruined, a beautiful art spoiled. From that depth springs our desire for beauty and our sense that something has gone dreadfully wrong. Because we are still bearers of God's image, we have some idea of how things should be, how the song should go, what the painting should look like. And yet because that image in us has been tainted by our sin, we recognize when there is injustice, we know that the song is being sung out of tune, that the painting has been smeared, that all is not as it should be.

The story does more than give us an explanation of the human condition. It offers a picture of God that we never thought possible. Most religious stories get their shape by a person's search for God. A certain prophet wandered off in the wilderness in search of God. Or a wise philosopher climbed the mountain to ponder truth. Or the old sage began a quest for contact with the Being in the Sky.

But the Jewish-Christian story does not begin with a man or woman searching for God. Quite the contrary. When the image-bearers realize that their attempt at living independently of their Creator has tainted His image in them, they recognize for the first time their frail and vulnerable state. "I was afraid because I was naked; so I hid," Adam said (Gen. 3:10). Man and woman are not searching for God; they are hiding from Him, hoping to avoid Him altogether. It is God then who said to Adam, "Where are you?" (Gen. 3:9).

The magnitude of that question cannot be overstated. There are many ancient creation myths, from the Babylonians and Egyptians who neighbored the ancient Israelites, to the Chinese and Indians in Asia, from Native Americans to Africans. All the oldest civilizations have versions of how the world began. Some suggest a god vomited up the earth and sun. Others say a god won a bloody war and formed the corpse of his foe into our universe. There are tales of erotic escapades of the deities that spawned the worlds we now know, and legends of cosmic betrayal, sorcery, and incest. But these stories show gods who created the earth as their playground with humans as their toys, or creation as a sort of unintended consequence or subplot to their main drama. The Jewish-Christian story is unique in its depiction of a personal God who set out to make the world, a God who means to create and, in the midst of creating, calls it good. Not incidental or accidental. *Good.* This is not a capricious, angry, warring god who seeks to destroy the wicked man and woman for their rebellion. This is a God who comes looking. The God who calls out to Adam, "Where are you?"

The fallen image-bearers were expelled from Eden, but the quest to redeem them—indeed the whole creation—had already begun.

The Original Luck-Bearers

From the beginning, God. God who is calling, God who is choosing, God who is blessing. Adam had been blessed by God, commissioned to multiply, to fill the earth with other image-bearers so that the world would be filled with the glory of God. Adam chose to attempt autonomy instead. Adam's descendants are a mixed garden of grass and weeds; there are those who listened to God's call, some with remarkable intimacy like Enoch, and those who ignored it, some with astounding audacity like Cain.

The rebellion of the image-bearers reached a condensation point, and the sky became heavy with God's judgment. It rained and rained and rained. When Noah and his family, singled out by

God to survive these torrents, set foot on a land ready to bloom with new life, God reissued His blessing on the remnants of His original creation: multiply, cover the earth with men and women who know God and reflect His image. Noah filled the earth, but with more fallen image-bearers. Some of these fallen image-bearers even reversed their call to reflect God and made up gods after their own image instead.

God was going to show the world what He was like, and He would do it from within His creation, fallen though they were. And He began it slowly, with one family, one that the rest of the world could watch, a family through whom all other families could be blessed.

So God blessed Abraham. Abraham's blessing was special. It wasn't simply to re-create, to multiply. It was a call to carry the blessing to others—indeed to the world. To be clear about His plan, God didn't stop with blessing Abraham; He blessed Abraham's son, Isaac, and He blessed the son who got Isaac's blessing, Jacob, through the man who wrestled with him until daybreak. The ones who received this blessing are forever remembered when this God is named: the God of Abraham, Isaac, and Jacob.

As the seed of Abraham multiplied, they did the blessing, passing on what Yahweh had given them. They were not merely fallen image-bearers; they were to be luck-bearers. They carried God's blessing, and they were to bring it to the world.

In Frederick Buechner's novel of Jacob's life, he describes the moment that Jacob, far from home, toiling under his uncle's manipulative oversight, realizes the significance of his children, born from four different mothers,[2] but of the same seed:

I was like a man caught out in a storm with the
wind squalling, the sand flailing me across the eyes,
the chilled rain pelting me. The children were the
storm, I thought, until one day, right in the thick of
it, I saw the truth of what the children were.

One boy was pounding another boy's head
against the hard-packed floor. Another was drows-
ing at his mother's [breast]. Three of them were
trying to shove a fourth into a basket. Dinah was
fitting her foot in her mouth. The air was foul with
the smell of them.

They were the Fear's promise.[3] That is what I
suddenly saw the children were. I had forgotten it.
They were the dust that would cover the earth. The
great people would spring from their scrawny loins.
Kicking and howling and crowing and … slobber-
ing food all over their faces, they were the world's
best luck.[4]

The world's best luck. The world's best chance of being renewed,
of being restored with their Creator, would come through this
nation, this people, Israel.

Later in Buechner's novel, Joseph tells Pharaoh how his God
speaks, calls, still calling, all those years after calling out after the
fallen image-bearers in Eden:

He speaks to us sometimes in dreams that are like
torches to light our way in through the dark.… He

> gives us daughters and sons so that our seed may
> live after us and the promises he has made us may
> be kept to the world's luck and blessing.[5]

There were moments in Israel's history when they seemed to grasp that they were not chosen for themselves. They were chosen for the sake of others. "The 'chosen' ... are chosen ... for the sake of the unchosen,"[6] C. S. Lewis wrote. The fallen image-bearers God called have become lucky, for God has spoken to *even such as these*. But the luckless are made lucky so that they might be luck-bearers to the world.

Nevertheless this nation, this people chosen to carry luck to the world, failed to keep listening to the Creator. Much of what we call the Old Testament is the story of Israel trying to live out their calling to bring God's blessing to the world. There were glimmers of remarkable radiance, when they were a light unto the nations, when an ancient queen visited the wealthy Solomon and pronounced, "Lucky the men and women who work for you, getting to be around you every day and hear your wise words firsthand! And blessed be GOD, your God, who took such a liking to you and made you king. Clearly, GOD's love for Israel is behind this, making you king to keep a just order and nurture a God-pleasing people" (1 Kings 10:8–9 MSG).

There were times when Israel's farmers refused to overharvest their fields so that those without land could glean from the corners and be fed, days when those who had no home could join Israel and become part of her nation, an unthinkable idea for a region steeped in tribalism and family ties.

And yet there were moments when they set up golden images borrowed from their pagan neighbors and called them Yahweh. They confused and fused the religions and practices of their day. They forgot that, when God told them to have no other gods, He was telling them that He was enough for them. They couldn't believe it, they thought they needed more, something else, some other god they could use to secure their wishes and control their outcomes. By insisting on shaping God's image to be an amalgam of deities—mixing a little Baal, a little Molech, a little Yahweh—they were repeating the sin of their first father and mother: They were becoming a god unto themselves.

The Invasion

Before the beginning, God. God, the Three in One, who sees the end from the beginning. God, who decided before the foundations of the world that Christ the Son would be the Lamb of God, slain for the sin of the world.

God was not caught off guard by Adam's sin. He knew His first image-bearers would taint His image in them by their own rebellion. He knew the people He chose to be His luck-bearers would instead become self-absorbed and syncretistic. He knew they would become a curse, a byword among the nations instead of a blessing to all peoples. He knew their eventual exile out of the Promised Land, like Adam and Eve's expulsion from Eden, would only underscore the plight of all creation: a luckless world waiting for redemption, a redemption that could only come from beyond itself.

And so He came.

Christ entered into the luckless, joyless, lifeless world. He was born to the unlikeliest of people: a Jewish carpenter and his ordinary wife. Yet even His arrival in her womb elevated her. Because of Him, she, the scandal of her town, the subject of scornful whispers and smirking eyes, was called by an angel "highly favored … among women" (Luke 1:28 NKJV). She was *blessed*. Though they did not know it yet, the luckless had become lucky.

At His birth, shepherds—rootless wandering rogues—were visited by a choral constellation of angels announcing good news. Like Abraham, the nomadic shepherd God had visited thousands of years earlier; like Moses, the shepherd in Midian tending his father-in-law's flock, who saw a bush on fire yet not consumed; like David, the king God crowned while he was hidden in the valley tending his father's sheep—shepherds are once again the lucky ones, the ones God visits. Something about them must remind Him of Himself. Although dirty and stained, His image in them still shimmers in the light of His glorious eyes.

Jesus, from His conception and birth, began bringing blessing to the world. This was the fulfillment of what God had promised Abraham. God had promised to bring blessing to the world through Abraham's family; now the promise was coming to pass specifically through Jesus the Messiah. Jesus is Abraham's seed, the Chosen One, the One who would perfectly fulfill the call to reveal God to the world and to rescue and restore all created things. He is the perfect Image-Bearer, for He is "the image of the invisible God" (Col. 1:15).

Not only is Jesus the perfect Image-Bearer, He is also the ultimate Luck-Bearer. Through His life, death, and resurrection, humanity will be redeemed, and creation will be restored. Humanity had been wasting away since the first man, by his disobedience, brought death into the world. But now, through this "one man's obedience," life—unexpected, undeserved, abundant, overflowing Life, the Life of the age to come!—would come to all (Rom. 5:19; see 12–20 ESV).

Walking the shores of Galilee, the God who called Adam out of hiding began calling people out of their small, self-destructing lives. "Stop this attempt at autonomy. Stop trying to be better, do better, on your own. Stop casting your nets and toiling all night and hoping for different results. It is futile. You cannot live without Me. You were not made to. Come. Follow Me."

As He healed the sick and drove out demons, He was signaling the arrival of His kingdom. It was an invasion. But not an invasion of a foreign army; rather it was the arrival of creation's rightful King. His rule was undoing the infection of evil. With every miracle, He was announcing that the jig was up, the time had come. History was now turning on a hinge.

Isaiah's vision of Messiah hundreds of years earlier was of one who, by His own wounds, would heal the fractures (Isa. 53): in Israel, the nation torn apart by idolatry and sin; in the world, which had fallen into a constant state of war; in humanity, which found itself irreparably distant from God. Messiah would lead to swords being beaten into plowshares and spears into pruning hooks; war would be retired forever. Beasts and humans would live in harmony (Isa. 2:4; 11:6–8). The prophets tell of a Messiah who would take this world, sick and broken and fractured and fallen, and make it whole, set it right.

In His death and resurrection, Jesus did just that. At the cross Jesus carried upon Himself every sin, every rebellion of the entire race of image-bearers. And in doing so, He redeemed not only them but the whole cosmos they had knocked out of kilter. By taking the full weight of sin—by "becoming sin," becoming the curse—and then rising up from the grave, He defeated sin and reversed the curse of death. He set creation on a new trajectory, one that creation itself longs for (Rom. 8:19–25), one bound for renewal: a new heaven and a new earth (Rev. 21:1–5). As in the beginning, so in the end: God.

Because Jesus is the long-awaited fulfillment of the old promise, God, the "God of Abraham, Isaac, and Jacob," is called, first by Paul and Peter, "God the Father of our Lord Jesus Christ." Jesus, the Son of God, creation's rightful King and the world's true Lord, had broken the stain of the rebellion, ended the luckless night that had fallen upon earth, and with His resurrection, awakened a new dawn, giving us hope for the fullness of day that will come when He returns and all things will be made new and the cosmos set right.

This is why Jesus came. And He knew it.

So when Jesus opened His mouth to speak, He was making an announcement, the announcement His life itself proclaimed: "Good news! God has come … even to such as these! Luck has come to a luckless world. The kingdom of God has come to unlikely people."

Rethinking the Kingdom

Here we must stop and ask, "But what is the kingdom of God?" You hear the phrase thrown about in Christian circles frequently. "Let's build the kingdom of God," people sometimes say. Or, "We're working to expand God's kingdom!" Is it surprising to know that we are not asked to do either of those things in the Scriptures?

So what, then, is the kingdom of God? It would be difficult to summarize all the dimensions of the kingdom here. There is broad agreement among scholars of the Scriptures, though, that the kingdom in its essence is the "rule of God." One of the twentieth century's best expositors of kingdom theology in the New Testament, the late George Eldon Ladd, notes, "The *primary* meaning of both the Hebrew word *malkuth* in the Old Testament and of the Greek word *basileia* in the New Testament is the rank, authority and sovereignty exercised by a king."[7] While *basileia* may at times refer to a realm where that rule is expressed or a people over whom that rule is exercised, a kingdom is first of all "the authority to rule, the sovereignty of the king."[8]

God's kingdom, then, is His rule expressed through His people, the ones He is in covenant with. His covenant with Adam and Eve was for them to express God's rule as they brought God's wise, loving order to His good creation. The kingdom of God on earth is a pre-fall idea. Regardless of the popular and often overly romanticized sayings that God made us to worship Him or to be His lovers, Genesis tells us that God made humans in His image and said, "Let them reign!" (Gen. 1:27–28). If that is what is meant by saying that we were made to worship God—that we look like God and reflect His rule on earth—then all is well. But I suspect that we have forgotten about being made as God's image-bearing rulers of His good creation and have turned worship into a syrupy emotional experience and a word that has lost all real meaning. Adam and Eve were to be His image-bearing rulers. Yes, friendship, relationship, and intimacy are all built into this, but it may be help-ful to think of their vocation as a sort of priestly and kingly one. Yet they failed. Again God's covenant with Noah was to express God's rule on the earth after the flood. He, too, was flawed. God's covenant with Abraham—and by extension with Israel—was for them to be a people that would live in a way that expressed God's rule and bring the blessings of that rule to other nations. They were to be a kingdom of priests. They too fell short.

But God knew what was coming. The plan all along was to keep His covenant people roughly on course like a train on the tracks until the perfect Israelite came. Jesus the Messiah kept covenant fully and faithfully. He was fully Priest and King. N. T. Wright, one of our generation's most brilliant theologians, writes on how Jesus confronted and defeated evil by His dual role of King and Priest "through Israel's Messiah fighting the battle for the kingdom through his own suffering and death, and through Israel's true priest offering Israel's God the obedient sacrifice at the heart of the new Temple."[9]

Wright continues, explaining how Jesus ultimately fulfilled the call of Adam to reflect God's image and bring God's order. Luke traces Jesus' genealogy to Adam to at least help us see this connection. Paul makes it clearer in his letter to the Romans, contrasting Jesus, through whom life comes to all, with Adam, through whom death came to all. But Jesus, Wright argues, is also the direct fulfillment of the call of Abraham and Israel, the people chosen to bless the world and bring about its rescue. This is what Paul is trying to tell us in both Romans and Galatians, when he references Abraham. It is also the reason for Matthew's genealogy

of Jesus that goes back to Abraham. Again, *Jesus is Abraham's seed!*
Wright explains:

> Jesus is announcing the kingdom and is himself
> the true though very surprising king, [and is also]
> embodying the true Temple and is himself the true
> (though shocking) high priest. Jesus thus embod-
> ies the two great narratives of Israel, the royal and
> the priestly strands of the Old Testament, drawing
> them together and establishing the new way, the
> royal and the priestly way, for Israel and for the
> human race, for the sake of the world.[10]

Jesus' arrival marked the fullest expression of the kingdom of
God on earth up until that point. The rule of God has come in
Christ. When Jesus comes again, the rule of God will come in ultimate fullness. He will set everything right. God will be King not only
de jure, by right, but *de facto,* by reality.

The rule of God is seen, then, as a present reality (Matt. 12:28),
and yet also a future hope (1 Cor. 15:24, 50). God's rule is an inward
righteousness, peace, and joy that we experience in the Holy Spirit
(Rom. 14:17), but it will also one day be an outward political triumph
in which every earthly rule gives way to God's rule (Rev. 11:15).
The rule of God is something we enter now (Matt. 21:31–32; Heb.
12:28), and yet a place we will enter later (Matt. 8:11; 1 Cor. 6:9–10;
Gal. 5:19–21; 2 Thess. 1:5). It is something we can, indeed must,
receive now (Mark 10:15), and also something we will receive in the
future (2 Peter 1:10–11).

These tensions are what Ladd and others have described as the kingdom that has come "now but not yet." The tension is seen in passages like Romans 8:18–25 and 1 Corinthians 15, where creation groans for the return of Christ and evil is finally destroyed and defeated. The tension is also what we wrestle with in prayer: "Your kingdom come … on earth as it is in heaven" (Matt. 6:10). We know that God's rule is not fully realized here on earth; there is much that is not the way God intended. The world is broken, fractured, sick, diseased. Yet God has acted to heal it. He has entered our suffering, shared our affliction, taken upon Himself the full weight of evil, and destroyed it completely. Evil has been put on notice: The true King of creation and of the world has come. And He will come again. And when He does, it's game over. His rule will fully be expressed. He will rule, He *must* rule, "until he has put all his enemies under his feet" (1 Cor. 15:25). And "the last enemy to be destroyed is death" (v. 26).

This is the hope of the entire Old Testament. Every time the psalmist cries out, "The Lord reigns!" he is proclaiming that Yahweh-God, the Creator of the heavens and the earth, is sovereign over all. Yet laced throughout the Psalms and the Prophets is an awareness that all is not as God intended. A good creation has been spoiled; the painting has been tainted; the song is being sung off-key. The cry "The Lord reigns!" becomes not simply proclamation but also petition: "Come and reign! Come and rescue the world! Come and set it right!" It is the hope Zechariah the prophet anticipated when he wrote, "The LORD will be king over the whole earth. On that day there will be one LORD, and his name the only name" (Zech. 14:9).

Future Tense

Here we are in the middle. The kingdom has come, but it has not yet come in fullness. Our tendency is to ask what we can do to *make* it come in fullness. What can we do? How can we bring it? How can we have it *now?*

It is a little like a boy who has discovered, in early December, that his father has bought him a bicycle for Christmas. Imagine if that boy comes to his father and says, "Dad, you paid for that bike."

"Yes, son, yes I did," the father replies.

"Then Dad, because I am your son and because you have paid for it, I receive it now in the name of Smith [assuming this is their family name]."

"But son, it's not Christmas," the father answers in amusement.

"Dad, you paid for my bike," the boy insists.

"Yes …" The father hesitates.

"So I receive it now in the name of Smith!" The boy is now getting quite worked up—fervent, you might say, in his request. It has taken on a tone of *authority*. He *knows who he is*. But it doesn't change the plan.

"Son, I am your father, and I love you very much. And I have paid for this bike in full. But it is your Christmas present. Now wait until Christmas Day. In the meantime, enjoy the helmet and begin to imagine what it will be like to have this bike. Prepare for it. Plan the routes you will ride. Get ready. But wait."

You can see I am poking a little bit at the various preachers you may have heard on TV who, in earnest ignorance, teach us to simply "claim" things from God in Jesus' name. That kind of talk displays a lack of understanding of the kingdom. It has come and it is coming.

But while some may miss an important truth of the kingdom of God by insisting on everything here and now, others react by going too far the other way. Out of a pure desire to make our worship and allegiance to Jesus be for "who He is and not what He does," they obliquely suggest that God is unmoved by our plight. *It doesn't matter if God heals you or not, just worship Him.* Or, *If God doesn't provide or come through, then so be it. He's God and you're not!* We've heard these things, and there is certainly truth to these lines. But it can leave us feeling that God is distant and uncaring, that His answer to our requests is "not here, not now, and maybe not ever." But what are we to make of the multitude of God's promises and the thick hymnal of Israel's prayers? Psalm 20 is just one example of God's people crying out to a God whom they believed cared very much about their physical state and their plans and battles and petitions. And He does care! That is the whole point of His making a covenant with them.

One attempt to resolve the tensions implicit in a caring God who seems to not act is to suggest that heaven is where God really has His way. The kingdom of God is neither all here and now nor is it not here, not now, not ever. It is, by this account, simply "not here and not now." Later all will be well, when God takes us out of here. In this view, wildly popular in the second half of the last century, salvation is an evacuation plan, and the kingdom of God has no bearing upon the earth, God's original creation. But what, then, are we to make of the prayer *Jesus* told us to pray: "Your kingdom come, Your will be done, on earth as it is in heaven"?

A full reading of the Scriptures reveals that the kingdom of God *is* to come to earth. It is, in other words, about the "here."

God cares about all that is wrong with His creation, with His earth, with His creatures, with His humans. He is moved by our disease and our poverty and our suffering. And He intends to set things right *here*. As we explore Luke's Beatitudes, you will see that Jesus is announcing that the kingdom of God is coming *here*. Things will be different; indeed they are already becoming different. There is a "now" aspect to the kingdom. The reversal has, in fact, begun. For the poor, the kingdom is theirs. For the persecuted, their reward is great. But the fullness of the kingdom is yet to come. Those who are weeping here will be comforted. Those who are hungry now will be filled. You might say that the kingdom of God is *here* but not fully *now*. Or that the kingdom of God is *here* and *now* but *not yet*.

Back to our question: How do we live in this tension of the "now but not yet"? What should we do? What can we do?

First off, we must know this: We cannot *bring* the kingdom; only Christ can when He comes again. So then, what are we to do in the meantime? We are to do what Jesus told His disciples to do: announce the arrival of the kingdom. The true King of the world has come. Let the earth rejoice! More than merely making a verbal declaration, we are to live in surrender to Jesus as if we truly believe He is the King of the world. We are to learn to live in the kingdom now so that when it comes in fullness, remaking earth and heaven, we will truly be at home. In other words, here on earth in the meantime, we are to announce the kingdom's arrival and to anticipate its culmination. Both of these things, the announcing and the anticipating, are the subjects of this book as we explore the Beatitudes in Luke 6.

In Christ

But before we turn our attention there, we must recognize that something has happened to us now because of Jesus. Because He faithfully kept the covenant, He fulfilled the calling on Adam and Noah, but more precisely, the covenant with Abraham, Isaac, and Jacob. And because He did, and we are in Christ, we, like Adam, like Noah, like Abraham, Isaac, and Jacob, are now blessed. *We* are "blessed … in the heavenly realms with every spiritual blessing in Christ" (Eph. 1:3).

In Christ, *we* are now the covenant people of God.

In Christ, the image of God is now being restored in us. *We* are now "the righteousness of God" (2 Cor. 5:21).

In Christ, our commission to cover the earth with the glory of God—to multiply image-bearers—is recovered. We are now "Christ's ambassadors" (2 Cor. 5:20).

This *Luck* is far more than getting a work visa to stay on in America; this is about being made citizens of the kingdom. This *Luck* is much more than receiving a great inheritance and therefore great expectations; this is about being made heirs with Christ of a new creation that God is working to bring about.

In Christ, we have become *lucky* so we can become God's image-bearers and His luck-bearers to the world. The kingdom of God has come *to* us so that it might come *through* us to others. We are carriers of the kingdom, the arrival of which Jesus ushered in, the kingdom He inaugurated by His arrival and will culminate at His return. The kingdom of God, the rule of God, is still being expressed on earth through the covenant people of God. And it is bringing restoration, rescue, order to all things. It is setting things right.

If we are to be such carriers, if we are to live in a way that anticipates the kingdom coming, we must know the values of this kingdom. Since we have been lavished with such love, such blessing, such *Luck,* we must learn how to live in this new way. We must let the King have His way in us and work this life out in us. So we turn to look more closely at the ones whom the King calls lucky.

DISCUSSION QUESTIONS

1. Have you ever received an anonymous gift and been unsure of why it was given or what to do with it?

2. Based on this chapter, how would you describe what the kingdom of God is?

3. In your life, how have seen the truth of the kingdom "already but not yet" come in its fullness?

4. What do you think it means to say that the "kingdom has come to you so that the kingdom can come through you"? In what ways can you live that out?

CHAPTER THREE

THE GOD-DEPENDENT

We weren't poor.

At least that's not how I remember it. None of my emotions from those three years has any shade of lack, any hue of disappointment. I remember being excited to go over to my friend Deryk's house because he had a basketball hoop in his driveway and a TV that actually worked. I liked when I went to the house of another friend who had a Super Nintendo and we played Contra all Saturday morning. There were some days I wished I had a Super Nintendo. But I never felt poor.

My feelings, even the ones that have survived over two decades of my life from then until now, were happy and warm, memories of family togetherness, of an adventure we had collectively embarked upon. It's the facts, which have also survived the time, that my adult imagination can't reconcile with those feelings.

The facts were that in 1988, when my family moved from Malaysia to Portland, Oregon, so that my parents could obey

God's call and attend Bible college, we left a life of relative comfort. In Malaysia my father was an account executive at a big ad agency that provided a company car and a membership to a modest country club. When we moved to America, his student visa prevented him from gaining employment outside the Bible college or its host church. So he took a job as a janitor. It paid $4.50 an hour and came with the added perk of letting me shoot hoops in the gym while my dad vacuumed the hallways late at night. Our apartment was furnished with couches that a thrift store might have thrown out, either for their putrid faded orange upholstery or for the flattened foam that pressed thinly against old spring coils. Someone gave us a bicycle that my dad rode to the grocery store a few blocks away. Balancing multiple paper sacks while trying to steer proved hazardous on at least one occasion, as we learned when my dad came home with a small cut on his forehead after running into a wall. When we finally shelled out $450 for a graying Toyota that we thought was a godsend, we realized the greater miracle would be getting it to start on a winter morning. But it did. Every time.

I never thought we were poor. My parents never said we were. Neither did my friends. It wasn't until I graduated from college and started earning my own modest paycheck that I began to question how we survived those years. Now, as a husband, a father of three, carrying the weight of responsibility for my own family, I have a hard time imagining those first years in America. *How did we make it? Why were we so happy? Why is it that all I remember is talking and laughing with my sister and my mother and my father?*

In those years, everything was a gift. Once a neighbor knocked on our door and offered us a pizza that they had not been able to finish after feeding the folks who helped them move in. Our eyes bulged as our faces broke into silly grins. We might as well have been offered dinner at the Ritz. Only moments earlier we had been joking about how nice it would be to order a pizza for dinner. It was a joke because we knew we couldn't have afforded it. Everything was a gift. Pizza Hut was manna from heaven.

Unlikely Cover Models

It would have surprised Jesus' listeners when He announced that the poor are blessed. Good Jews were raised to believe that if God blessed you, you would not be poor. Some version of this logic is what Job's friends applied to him when calamity hit. Job, they insisted, must have sinned, must have offended God. In the same way, prosperity, not poverty, was the supposed mark of God's blessing. In Psalm 144:13–15, the psalmist exclaims:

> *Our barns will be filled*
> *with every kind of provision.*
> *Our sheep will increase by thousands,*
> *by tens of thousands in our fields;*
> *our oxen will draw heavy loads.*
> *There will be no breaching of walls,*
> *no going into captivity,*
> *no cry of distress in our streets.*

> *Blessed are the people of whom this is true;*
> *blessed are the people whose God is the LORD.*

The psalmist is not alone in equating material prosperity with divine blessing. Roughly two millennia after the psalmist wrote those words, Martin Luther critiqued the underlying belief of the Roman church that the one who is rich and powerful is the one who is blessed. Luther called it "the most universal belief or religion on earth," one on which "all men depend according to their flesh and blood," making it impossible to "regard anything else as blessedness."[1]

Even the ancient Greeks shared this view of the "blessed." In their versions of beatitudes, seen in their prose and poetry throughout the centuries, the people they called blessed were the parents for their children, the rich for their wealth, the wise for their wisdom, and the pious for their virtue. And the word they used for their blessing was the same word Jesus used in Luke 6—*makarios*.[2]

Such thinking persists. We still think that the ones who are living in godlike bliss are the ones who have all the money, the brilliance, the virtue, and the kids who are doing well. *Those* are the lucky ones.

The people who adorn the covers of magazines, the ones who get interviewed on TV, the men and women who are held up before us to admire and emulate are the rich, the powerful, the successful. Our suspicion that those people are better off than we are is confirmed by the images and stories and sounds that flood our minds and eyes and ears. Even many Christians uncritically regard financial improvements as blessings from God. A promotion, a new house, a new car, an unexpectedly successful investment decision; these are all what we would call blessings. And, to an extent, rightfully so. It is good to give thanks to the Lord. It is good to credit Him with our increase, as Moses reminded the children of Israel to do when they entered the Promised Land. Gratitude is a way of remaining God-reliant.

But this unchallenged, simplistic, absolute association of divine blessing with material abundance is not without its dangers. It can, as Luther argued, lead us to greed. It can also make us hold up the wrong man or the wrong woman as the one whom God has blessed. We can say to ourselves, "Aha! That person is blessed! That is what the blessed life looks like!" and we can be quite wrong.

Imagine if, by some fluke, the images from a *National Geographic* cover landed on the cover of *Esquire* or *Fortune*. What if under the headline "The Most Powerful Man in the World" was, by some bizarre mistake, a picture of an Afghani boy with a mud-stained face and fearful eyes? This startling incongruence of what we are used to thinking of as lucky and what is now being hailed and applauded would not be unlike the jarring dissonance of the previous Jewish notion of the blessed life and the life Jesus was calling blessed. Those who heard Jesus' words that day on the plain must have been bewildered and shocked. And curious.

Why would Jesus call the poor lucky?

We must resist the urge to jump to the spiritual answer. Luke's bare rendering "Blessed are the poor" doesn't allow us to immediately christen the first Beatitude as a euphemism for repentance. There is a pitfall on the other side too. Ignoring the essence of who the poor are, some have sought to make a virtue out of poverty itself, claiming the Lord's blessing on such a life. This too misses the point.

The very first thing we must remind ourselves of is that, at some level, Jesus is illustrating the paradox of the gospel of the kingdom: It has not come to the ones you would have supposed. It has come to even such as these. They are not, in the first place, being praised for being poor; they are receiving an unlikely announcement that, in spite of being the lowly and powerless, they are receiving the kingdom of heaven. Martin Luther, careful to make neither poverty nor prosperity the point, says that Christ is exhorting His followers: "If they are a failure, if they have to suffer poverty and do without riches, power, honor, and good days, they will still be blessed and have not a temporal reward, but a different, eternal one; they will have enough in the kingdom of heaven."[3] The blessing is in what they are receiving. The poor—the ones who are marginalized by society—are the ones who will enjoy God's rule. They get to participate in what God is doing; they will have a part in bringing His order and setting things right. For that, they are indeed lucky.

And yet …

Meeting the Poor

There is something Jesus wants us to see in His stunning announcement that the poor are blessed. Just as He caught the crowd's attention when He brought a little child before them and said that unless they were like him they would not enter the kingdom, so in this use of the poor to discuss inheriting the kingdom, Jesus is making a conspicuous point. There is something about the poor that He wants us to notice.

In the Old Testament, "the poor" refers to those who are materially poor, the destitute. The Torah is teeming with reminders of how to care for the poor, how to be mindful of them and never exploit them. But reading requires more than dictionary definitions. As we immerse ourselves in Israel's story, we see that soon "the poor" becomes not merely a reference to a certain category based on economic status; it becomes a metaphor for the powerless. In Leviticus, God instructs Israel to never treat a brother like a slave even if a person's poverty drives him to sell himself to another (Lev. 25:39). If a person hired a poor person—whether an Israelite or a foreigner—he should pay him before the sun goes down, for the poor man is depending on it to survive (Deut. 24:14–15). "The poor" now has a face. It is not a category or a designation. It is *that* person who is so desperate she is trying to sell herself as your slave; it is *that* man whom you hired who is counting on today's wage for his daily bread. *The poor* is the powerless, the one who depends on another for his own survival.

As we go on through the Old Testament and allow the prayers and songs of Israel to shape our imaginations, we see another twist in who the poor are. "The poor" is no longer a way of looking at a demographic of Israel's society; it becomes a way of describing the plight of Israel herself. Israel, overrun by enemies, attacked by bandits, threatened by the expanding empires of Assyria and Egypt and Babylon, is the marginalized and the oppressed. *She* is the poor. "Contend, O Lord, with those who contend with me," David prayed; "fight against those who fight against me. Take up shield and buckler; arise and come to my aid.… Then my soul will rejoice in the Lord and delight in his salvation. My whole being will exclaim, 'Who is like you, O LORD? You rescue the poor from those too strong for them, the poor and needy from those who rob them'" (Ps. 35:1–2, 9–10).

But in the prayers and songs of Israel, we also see another, deeper layer. We have understood the poor as the powerless. We have recognized that the people of God are not exempt from such status, that they too find themselves besieged and surrounded and in situations beyond their control; they too are poor. Now we see beyond the surface: In the Psalms, the poor are the God-dependent. This reality has been there all along. It was God, Yahweh, who gave instructions to Israel about how to treat the poor, the alien, the foreigner, the ones who had no means of providing for themselves. He was their Defender, seeing ahead of their need and making provision for it through His people, always taking special note of those who had come to the end of their rope. In the Psalms—in prayer and worship—the poor freely admit their dependence on God:

> *This poor man called, and the LORD heard him;*
> *he saved him out of all his troubles. (Ps. 34:6)*

> *Yet I am poor and needy;*
> *may the Lord think of me.*
> *You are my help and my deliverer;*
> *O my God, do not delay. (Ps. 40:17)*

> *Defend the cause of the weak and fatherless;*
> *maintain the rights of the poor and oppressed.*
> *(Ps. 82:3)*

*I know that the L*ORD *secures justice for the poor*
and upholds the cause of the needy. (Ps. 140:12)

*Who is like the L*ORD *our God,*
the One who sits enthroned on high,
who stoops down to look
on the heavens and the earth?

He raises the poor from the dust
and lifts the needy from the ash heap;
he seats them with princes,
with the princes of their people.
He settles the barren woman in her home
as a happy mother of children.

*Praise the L*ORD. *(Ps. 113:5–9)*

Those who heard Jesus' opening words of blessing would have understood that when He said "the poor," He was talking about the powerless, the God-dependent—those who had no means of elevating themselves. This helps to explain the apparent discrepancy between Luke's phrase, "Blessed are the poor," and Matthew's phrase, "Blessed are the poor in spirit." The materially poor have learned to be poor in spirit; they have learned to be God-dependent. Steeped in the language of the Old Testament stories and prayers and songs, the two are nearly synonymous.

Jesus picked the poor as His poster people for those who are blessed by receiving the kingdom to tell us that full reliance upon God is what opens us up to His rule. The God-reliant, God-dependent are the ones who, as one commentary puts it, "gladly accept God's rule" and "enjoy the benefits."[4] In *The Message*, the first Beatitude reads, "You're blessed when you've lost it all. God's kingdom is there for the finding" (Luke 6:20 MSG).

The Land of the Self-Reliant

Right now, I'm sitting in a place you would recognize. You may have never been in this seat or this city, but you've likely been where I am. I'm in Starbucks. Happy music is playing, sunlight is streaming through the large panel windows, and I'm sitting with a drink, the name of which is almost as long as an Old Testament genealogy. (Tall, six-pump classic, breve, Awake tea latte.) Here my words have predictable outcomes. If I want something a particular way, I have the power to make it so. Here I am led to believe that the world can be custom fit to me. Here, if I have five dollars to spare, I can feel like a king, like I have the universe—and an exquisite drink—at my fingertips. Because Starbucks has become a massive multinational enterprise, I can go anywhere in the world— from small-town Iowa to big-city Kuala Lumpur, Malaysia—and have nearly the exact same experience at a Starbucks. And to be honest, I rather like it.

But it's an illusion. I am not really in control. Life never follows my order like a barista does. Maybe that's why I like coming to Starbucks. It makes me forget that I'm not always able to determine my outcomes, that most things are too complex or too far beyond my ability to fix. It's the American Illusion: If you make enough money, you can buy the life you want. You can purchase the right food, the right drugs, the right health care so that you can cheat death and disease over and over again; you can buy the right house in the right neighborhood with the right security system and gates so that you can avoid burglary or noise or too many cars in your cul-de-sac; you can vacation in all the right spots with people ready to attend to your every need as if you were an ancient Egyptian monarch. You can construct the illusion of a self-made man or woman. And you would be hailed for it. In America the first Beatitude is "Blessed are the self-reliant, the ones who are able to make something of themselves, for the best of this world is theirs."

It is affliction that wakes us from this illusion. The pain of a marriage breaking apart, a child wandering away from home, a disease whose onset can't be slowed, a retirement account that suddenly vanishes—these and more remind those in wealthy nations of what connects them with humanity at large: pain. In the end, it is our experience of pain, not our accumulation of prosperity, that joins us as the human race. In affliction we are reminded of our mortality, of our dependence on something other than ourselves. Poverty itself is no virtue, but poverty or affliction can be the occasion to realize that we are not in control.

The poor, because they have seen the good things of this life fall apart, because they have suffered affliction and seen how temporal the riches of this world are, have learned to accept that they are not king, they are not sovereign. And it is precisely this admission of their own lack of sovereignty that has opened them up to accept God's rule. They are set up to become God-dependent. Ultimately being *poor* has to do with our orientation toward God. It is a move away from self-reliance; it is a recognition of our God-dependence. It is finally realizing that self-confidence is not a kingdom value. We are not lucky for having much, nor are we lucky for having little. We are lucky when we learn to become completely God-dependent.

Bound By Prometheus

So how can we be God-dependent in an age of affluence? What if, at the present, there aren't experiences of pain or suffering that provide us with the opportunity to be God-reliant in a deeper sense?

The Greek myth of Prometheus provides a way. In one telling of the story, Prometheus, as a sort of revenge on Zeus, does three things to aid a human revolt. He first erases the memory in humans of the day of their death. Up until then, humans, according to Greek lore, were born with the knowledge of the day they would die, a built-in sense of limitation. Having removed their sense of finiteness, Prometheus then filled their heads with dreams larger than what they could achieve. Then to complete his mischief, he gave them fire. This last bit is the best-known part of the myth of Prometheus. But we would do well to pay attention to all three acts.

The modern man and woman have lost any sense of mortality or limitation. Our heads and hearts have been nourished on the lie from the Romantic era that we can be anything we want to be, that we can achieve anything we set out to achieve. And with every technological innovation—from the microchip to a globe wrapped with fiber-optic cable—we start to believe a little bit more that we *can* indeed do anything. We have fire in our hands, dreams in our hearts, and no concept of limitation in our heads.

And so we live. We tell our children they can be and do anything they set out to be or do. But it's a lie. It's an illusion that we have seen unravel as adults but still hope will be true for our children. We hope for them to make something of themselves that we couldn't make of ourselves. We live the illusion of self-reliance vicariously through our children. *Fire* is in our hands. But sooner or later, we will get burned.

We don't have to wait until we get burned. We can confess our limitations and the limitations of the things we have, the money we've earned, the stuff we've acquired. We can be honest and admit that a car will not make us invincible in bad weather, that a security system will not prevent a break-in, that a good investment strategy can't guarantee retiring as a millionaire. All these things are good, and they increase the probability of your desired outcomes. But they make no absolute promises. The simple act of acknowledging that can free you from a reliance on the wrong things.

It can also prevent you from disappointment when any of those things begin to crack. I know an airline pilot who lost a big chunk of his retirement after the airline filed for bankruptcy several years ago. He made adjustments to his family's plans and to their lifestyle and kept going. He knew the limitations of a corporate retirement plan. I know a young girl who is trying not to be disappointed when her boyfriend doesn't meet her every emotional need. She is learning about the limitations of human relationships. Everything on earth has limits.

The most difficult limitations to embrace are our own personal ones, the ceiling on our capacity. We have to put aside the foolish talk of boundless human potential and pray, as Moses did, that God would "teach us to number our days" (Ps. 90:12). All our efforts have limits. There are people we cannot help, situations we cannot change, goals we cannot achieve. We have limits. Embracing our finiteness helps us look up to the God who is infinite. Our boundedness opens us up to His boundless grace.

As we confess our limitations and number our days, we can choose to surrender our dreams. "Dreaming big" cannot be a virtue in itself; we cannot assume that any big dream must be God's dream because it is big. Dreams are for giving life to others. Joseph had to learn how to be a slave to Potiphar and a prisoner in Egypt before becoming a prince. In the difficult years, he learned to surrender his ambition and rejoice in someone else's success. It was then that he was lifted out of prison and put in the position to save his brothers and keep God's chosen family alive through years of drought.

We haven't yet understood this if our so-called big dreams make us ignore the small, simple moments. It never fails that the people who can't stop talking about spiritual things are the ones who can't seem to get their natural lives in order. The fantastic is an escape from the ordinary. They talk about wanting miracles to be the norm, but their family is in shambles. They put on a show on the platform but are rude to the volunteer who's driving them back to the hotel. Some of the meanest, most depersonalizing people are the ones consumed with their mission. I heard of a pastor who ruthlessly fired a faithful worship leader because he wanted someone who could help them "get where they wanted to go." When told of how hurt she was by the way he handled the situation, he gave some retort about this being a "spiritual war zone" and there not being time to worry about people's feelings. That is not the sort of talk that comes from the God-dependent. That is the language of self-importance, of the one who believes the weight of saving the world rests on his shoulders—the result of believing that your dreams are so urgent and divine that other people don't matter.

Confessing our limitations and surrendering our dreams helps us hold power loosely. We stop playing with fire. We understand that power corrupts, that even the noblest mortal will melt when held up too close to the sun. We must do with our power what Christ did with His: Give it away. Let others lead. Use the power you have to lift up others. This much we know. But to really ensure that the temptation of power has no grip on us, there are times when you must turn down a perfectly good opportunity. Sometimes taking on an additional role or responsibility is not about actually helping others; it's about gaining more status. That's when fire is in our hands. Let it go before you get burned.

To confess our limits, to surrender our dreams and embrace the ordinary, to hold power loosely and even turn down the chance to gain more—these are unlikely, uncommon spiritual disciplines that can help us remain God-dependent even in the midst of plenty. The God-dependent have learned that only God is fully in charge of the world He created. They understand that, even in plenty, all the good things of this life are simply a foretaste of what's coming. In the meantime the God-dependent know that everything here is a gift. Unexpected pizza is heavenly manna.

I Am Poor

There was a man who was looking for the kingdom. Sort of. He was blind. Nevertheless, with everything inside him, he was longing and *looking* for the rule of God to come. As a blind man in the first century, he was cast out onto the streets, perhaps because his family thought it was his sin that made God curse him with blindness. Either way, the blind in the first century were completely non-self-reliant. Society had done little to make basic survival possible for the handicapped. Pagans viewed them as weak, inferior to the healthy. Many Jews didn't improve the situation. The blind, the cripple, the lame were also the poor, the others-dependent. They could do little for themselves. They were reduced to begging.

Such was the case for Bartimaeus. He was a beggar, completely dependent on others for his survival. Every day he sat by the side of the road hoping he would get enough … food, drink, money, clothes … to make it through another day. Then one day, a crowd was going by. He heard whispers of the name *Jesus. The Jesus from Nazareth?* he thought. *The rabbi everyone has been talking about?*

Feet kept shuffling by him. Dirt was dancing around his skin. This was his moment. Bartimaeus cried out, "Son of David! Have mercy on me!"

Son of David. That was Messiah-talk. It referenced the ancient prophecy from Isaiah. Did Bartimaeus really think Jesus was *Messiah?*

His cry was met by the sound of angry voices. Male voices. Deep, gravelly barks. *Be quiet! Enough out of you! Don't trouble us!* He had heard those voices his whole life. Voices that pushed him aside, told him where to sit, to stand, voices that kept him on the margins. Raising his voice was the only way he could feel alive. Sending out sound waves of his own and letting them bounce off trees and bodies and sand and water was how he groped through a world of sounds.

So he raised his voice again. Louder this time. "Son of David! Have mercy on me!"

The shuffling feet stopped. A voice in the distance spoke. A male voice. But kinder, clear, and on purpose. *Call him,* the voice said. Then the gruff, male voices that earlier shoved him to the fringes spoke. Still deep and scolding. But the words were new: *Cheer up. Get on your feet. He's calling you.*

Fumbling, pushing himself against the ground with one hand, reaching out with another, Bartimaeus stumbled to his feet. With trembling fingers, his hands stretched out like a vine growing to the edges of the crowd; his knees, folding under the weight of his body, clumsily carried him toward the soft, tender voice.

The voice spoke again. *What do you want Me to do?* Why did Jesus ask that? Wasn't it obvious? Well, not exactly. A blind beggar could have asked for temporary help. He could have asked for bread, for water, for a new garment to replace his ragged, dirt-crusted one. But anyone could have given him that. There was something only God—or a man of God—could give Bartimaeus: his sight.

And so that was what he asked for. *Teacher, I want to see.* Bartimaeus' request revealed who he thought Jesus was. He couldn't have known yet that Jesus was the fully divine Son of God. But he knew enough to know that something about Jesus was God-like, that Jesus was somehow in touch with God in a way that he wasn't. And so he asked something of Jesus that only God could do. He asked for a miracle.

Jesus simply replied, "Your faith has healed you." It was like saying, "Bartimaeus, because you have begun to believe in who I am, because you recognize your lack of self-sufficiency, because you have asked for something that cuts to the root of your need, because you know the depth of your dependence on God, you will enjoy a taste of the rule of God now."

Healing is a foretaste of what the world will look like when God's rule culminates. We want the foretaste. We long to enjoy God's rule. But are we willing to confess our poverty, the bankruptcy in our hearts? Are we willing to admit that we are the blind, the poor, the beggar?

The words of Jesus to the church in Laodicea can be heard as they echo to us: "You say, 'I am rich; I have acquired wealth and do not need a thing.' But you do not realize that you are wretched, pitiful, poor, blind and naked" (Rev. 3:17).

Breaking in with a Bang

When you live fully reliant on God, you start to notice those who have no other hope besides God.

His name means "nation," but he could hardly provide for his family. Bang (pronounced "Bahng") has straight black hair that falls thickly over his forehead. His eyes are kind, and they shine now with gratitude. But Bang was once a man stripped of his dignity, humiliated by his inability to take care of his family. In Cambodia, as in many Asian cultures, it is shameful for a woman to be the sole breadwinner. Yet that was what Bang's wife was. And she wasn't winning that much bread. She was a police officer, a low-paying job in Cambodia, prone to the corruption of bribes.

Sak Saum means "dignity," and that's exactly what Eric and Ginny Hanson have brought to the people who work for them. As part of a larger ministry in Cambodia called In His Steps Cambodia, Sak Saum is a rehabilitation program for Cambodian women who have been rescued out of human trafficking. As they participate in the program, the women gain access to counseling, education, and specific training in job skills. Bit by bit, hope replaces despair, and dignity begins to rise.

When Ginny met Bang several years ago, she was the director of Sak Saum. Though Bang didn't fit the profile of the person they typically help, Ginny saw him. She recognized the hopelessness in his eyes. Here was a man who had no power to help himself. He was completely dependent. The trouble is, there was no one to really depend on.

Sak Saum decided to help Bang start a business, one that would work with a natural Cambodian resource that is in no short supply: coconuts. Bang is able to whittle and cut and polish and hone pieces of coconut into beautiful buttons and barrettes and key chains and musical instruments. His finished work is a deep and stunning brown that shines like his eyes now do.

As American missionaries living in Cambodia for almost a decade and a half, there is no doubt that Ginny and Eric have learned to be God-dependent. You could not survive otherwise. They are under no illusions of control. They have embraced their limitations, surrendered their dreams, and given their power away. And as a result, they are enjoying God's rule. They are resting in His control, trusting in His kingdom that has no end. But they have also become carriers of this kingdom hope. Because of their ministry, the kingdom of

God has broken into Bang's world. Once a poor man with no hope, he is now lucky.

Jesus saw Bartimaeus. Ginny saw Bang. Whom do you see? Every time you help the poor in Jesus' name, you are bringing the kingdom to them. You are making that place, that realm, reflect the rule of God. You are making things look the way they would if we allowed God to run the place. Because He is through you.

Lucky are the God-dependent, for they will enjoy and participate in God's rule.

DISCUSSION QUESTIONS

1. As an adult, have you ever had to depend on others for transportation or food or any other basic provisions? How did it make you feel?

2. Why is so difficult to admit that we are weak and poor, that we are fully dependent on God?

3. If Jesus asked you, "What do you want Me to do?" how would you respond?

CHAPTER FOUR

THOSE WHO ARE EMPTY ON THE WORLD

I couldn't believe we were going to eat at *that* restaurant. Not that I knew too much about it. I was thirteen or so at the time. But I knew it was fancy and expensive, and there would be lots of food. *Bring a sport coat*, my dad said. *A sport coat?* I repeated slightly confused. *Yes, that's the rule. You can't eat there in a T-shirt.* This was going to be some dinner.

Malaysians are famous for eating. All cultures boast that, I suppose, but Malaysians set out to prove it each night. Perfectly located between China and India, Malaysia is a melting pot of sorts for Southeast Asia. Over the years, as cultures collided and evolved into an amiable integration, new kinds of foods emerged. The spices and aromas of Indian cooking met the coconut and peanut influence of Thai cuisine; the ginger and garlic sauces of Chinese food mingled with the Malay art of wrapping meat in certain leaves for flavor. To be sure, there are Chinese restaurants and Indian restaurants and Malay restaurants and steak houses and Thai kitchens and so on. But the rich flavors of the region have combined in such a scintillating way that Malaysians can't help but eat round the clock. It would almost be a sin not to. The particular place we were going that night was a traditional Malaysian Chinese restaurant *par excellence*. A friend of my father's had invited us out, and while the usual get-togethers didn't include children, this time it was a family affair.

When we arrived, I discovered there would be nine courses. Nine! The opening round was the legendary shark's fin soup. The next eight were mostly a blur. Somewhere in there was an exquisite ginger beef dish, a Peking duck, a deep-fried and richly flavored fish, some sort of spicy chicken with peanuts, and king crabs in an exotic butter sauce. (I'm sure there were vegetable dishes too, but for some reason they have escaped my memory.) As a growing boy who had once been accused by my grandmother of having a python living in my stomach, I made the most of my seat at the table. You can usually measure how many rounds of food you've had in an Asian meal by how many bowls of rice you consumed with it. If the dishes are paint colors, then rice is the canvas; it is the backdrop for sensory delight. Five or six bowls of rice later, I was finally getting full. *Wow!* I thought. *This is the good life*. Here I was, not the reason for the feast, but a partaker nonetheless; not the guest of honor but a guest with full dining privileges.

And did I ever make full use of the privilege.

Messiah's Feast

When Jesus announced that those who are hungry now are blessed, He was likely talking about those who were literally struggling to eat. It's easy to imagine how the oppressive Roman regime made it difficult for a Jew to consistently provide for his family. What's more, the kinds of people who were gathered round listening to Jesus were not likely well fed. Luke tells us that many who were sick and troubled by unclean spirits had come to be healed and cured, and that Jesus had done just that before beginning to speak. These were people who, only moments ago, were sick and diseased and bothered by demons. Since this was a society in which the sick or the mentally troubled or demonically oppressed were cast to the fringes, many of them had been begging in order to eat. When Jesus said, "Blessed are *you* who are hungry now," He was looking at *them*. There in the crowd were ragged, rough, dirty beggars wearing big toothy grins because the diseases and the demons were gone.

But their bellies were likely still bloated from hunger. Why call *them* lucky? He wasn't toying with them. He was announcing the advent of a long-promised hope.

Jesus' first Beatitude in Luke gives a promise in the present tense: "yours is the kingdom of God" (6:20). The next two give a future hope. "Blessed are you who hunger now," Jesus said, "for you will be satisfied" (6:21).

Those words meant something to a Jew. They were steeped in Isaiah's vision of Messiah. He had spoken of a great feast that God would "prepare … for all peoples," a banquet with the "best of meats and the finest of wines" (Isa. 25:6). For the Jews in Jesus' day, they had been raised on the expectant hope that Messiah would one day answer His people and help them in the "day of salvation." He would "say to the captives, 'Come out,' and to those in darkness, 'Be free!'" (Isa. 49:9). God had promised that they would "feed beside the roads and find pasture on every barren hill"; they would "neither hunger nor thirst" (vv. 9–10). Jesus Himself would reference that particular text a few chapters later in Luke's gospel, saying that people would come from the "east and west and north and south" and "take their places at the feast in the kingdom of God" (Luke 13:29). The Jews of Jesus' day were living under Roman oppression, enduring hunger, waiting for God to finally rescue His people. When Jesus spoke of a future filling, He was awakening their longing for that day, the day when Messiah would come and bring His feast.

But here's the catch: There were many people listening to Jesus' announcements of blessing that day who didn't think they would be included in that feast. Surely that was for the exceptional, the heroic, the devout. Or simply the Jew.

A few chapters after Jesus' announcement of blessing on those who are hungry now, Luke tells of a man who says to Jesus, "Blessed is the man who will eat at the feast in the kingdom of God" (14:15). Jesus had just finished admonishing His dinner host, a prominent Pharisee, about what he should do when he throws a party. *Don't invite your friends or your relatives or your rich neighbors*, Jesus said. *Instead, invite the poor, the lame, blind, and the cripple—people who cannot repay you. Do that*, Jesus said, *and you will be blessed* (see Luke 14:12–14).

Ah, the man, himself a guest of the prominent Pharisee that night, said. *To be one of the people at the table for Messiah's feast! That person is blessed!*

But who is that person? Jesus then tells a story that gives more clues as to why He had told them to invite the poor, the lame, the blind, and the cripple—in short, the outcast—to their dinner parties. He tells of a man who was planning a big banquet and sent out invitations to many guests. Somehow they all have something better to do and turn him down. The master is angered by their callousness. *Fine*, he says to his servant. *Go out to the streets and alleys of the town and bring in the poor, the lame, the blind, and the cripple.* Then Jesus takes it one step further. *There's still room*, the servant says. *OK*, says the master. *Go out to the roads and the country lanes—the back roads!—and get anyone you can to come in so that my house can be full!*[1]

What is Jesus talking about? He is reclaiming Isaiah's vision of the feast being for *all* people. This is not just a banquet for Israel; this is a table set for *anyone* who will come. By using the "poor, the lame, the blind, and the cripple" in both His teaching and His story, Jesus was saying that the least likely people are exactly the ones who will feast at Messiah's table in the age to come. The honored, invited guests may be too proud to bother. But the lowly, the outcast, the forgotten, the ones who never get invited to anything, will—to everyone's surprise—be seated at this epic banquet.

You see, Luke tells us that among the crowd who gathered to listen to Jesus' sermon, His Beatitudes in chapter 6, were people from Tyre and Sidon, people who had no claim to covenant relationship with Israel's God. They were *outsiders,* the unlucky onlookers. By saying that those who are hungry now will be filled, Jesus was saying that they—yes, even they!—could partake of His feast. Jesus called the ones who were hungry in this world "lucky" because He knew they could partake of the feast that was coming, the feast in the age to come.

But Jesus also knew that the feast had begun. Here were the lame, the cripple, the poor gathered around Him now, feasting on

His teaching, nourished by His words and made healthy by His power. Messiah had come. Let the party begin.

Living with Hunger

When he answered my call, he didn't sound thrilled. He didn't sound angry either—just short, monotone responses in a heavy South Chicago accent. I was sort of expecting a warm, friendly voice ready to pick me up and take me to the convention. Trying to shake off the weariness of the day and focus my mind for a late-night workshop I was supposed to teach, I walked with urgency to the oversized baggage area and looked for my guitar. Not there. Worried that my ride might be getting perturbed with me for taking so long, I walked back to the regular baggage claim area to see if it would be coming around that carousel instead. There was my sturdy white case sliding down the belt. I grabbed my guitar with one hand and reached for my phone with the other, quickly redialing his number.

"Hey, Mike?"

"Yeah."

"This is Glenn...."

"..."

"Um ... I've got my stuff now ... and ... uh ... I'll be coming out of Vestibule 1B."

"1B?"

"Yes. Yes, sir."

"OK, I'll be there in a bit."

We shook hands, and he helped me load my stuff in the trunk. I opened the passenger door and couldn't help but notice the smell of tobacco in the car. *Is this just a limo service they hired? No. Can't be. He knows about the convention. There was something on the car about a "mission." I am speaking at a convention for Gospel Rescue Missions....*

"You're the third guy with a guitar I've picked up today," he said, interrupting my thoughts.

"Oh. Wow." My turn to be brief with responses. I was trying to figure out his story.

He asked a few questions about what I was going to be doing and where I lived. I found the nerve to ask a few questions about him. He was a driver. Picked up stuff from different locations all around a town about an hour away. Been at it for about a year. Grew up in South Chicago. Moved when he was a bit older then came back to the area as an adult.

"I like driving," he told me. Tapping the bill of his cap a bit lower on his forehead, he added, "I've got my hat, so I'm good to go."

There was something about his face, his expressions, his eyes that seemed like the face of a man who had been broken by pain. Not only pain that he experienced, but the pain that comes from seeing the pain you've caused someone else. It's a deep sort of pain that makes a man feel powerless over the course of time.

"I drive for a mission that takes in people who were alcoholics, drug addicts, and homeless. And I happen to fall in that category," he said without really looking at me.

I tried to affirm him, to tell him that I wouldn't have guessed, that his recovery seems to be going well, at least from my limited vantage point. As he told me more of his story, his wrinkled face began to show a bit more. He talked about the family members he had estranged and the grown daughter that kept cheering him on, albeit at times from a distance. He described years of being clean, but then intervals of devastating relapses. He described counselors who were helpful but whose help seemed incomplete because they weren't, in his words, "Jesus-based."

"It was just so hard. The more you do that stuff the more you start to believe that you can't stop, that you'll never get out of this. You feel stuck."

My eyes were already blurring with tears as my face mirrored his. He continued with a line that stopped me cold:

"I needed a strong God. A God that was strong enough to help me even when I'm alone … 'cause that's when I get into trouble."

Trying to empathize, I chimed in weakly, "Yeah … I mean, for all of us.…"

"Now when I'm alone, I just pray and call out to Jesus.… I open up my Bible … and He helps me, you know?"

"Yup." My head was bobbing like a conductor's wand, trying to take it all in. "That's awesome, man. What a journey you're on."

I was hungry, so we drove through a local hot dog place that he recommended, and the conversation tapered as I ate my food and made inane remarks about it really being a great hot dog. We were done. Enough soul-baring for one night.

Mike is empty on the world. The things that normally fill a person's life are mostly absent from his. He has hurt the ones he loves enough times that they are reluctant to trust him again. The home, the job, the things he once had are now gone. You might say he is an outsider, like the people from Tyre and Sidon who heard Jesus' words.

But Mike is lucky, for in spite of his emptiness he will be filled.

A Good Kind of Hungry

There is more to Jesus' blessing of the hungry. As much as Jesus is announcing the unexpected inclusion of unlikely outsiders to His table in the age to come, He is also applauding those who have not filled up on the world. Something about being hungry sets them up perfectly to be filled.

I can't shake my brief conversation with Mike, the recovering addict. I thought about it that night as I went to sleep and again the next day as I flew home. I'm still thinking about it. There is something about the face of a recovering addict. It's the same face you see on the village woman in a remote part of the world who can't feed her own children. It's the resigned look of deprivation, the face of someone who's learned to live with hunger. You see that same look on a recovering addict's face—only for them, it is not food they are living without.

For the addict who has been feeding on destructive substances or behaviors, the moment he begins to stop, there is a hunger for it, a craving that is hard to control. To continue living without that thing, the recovering addict doesn't hope for it to simply get easier or for the desires to go away. He learns instead to let that desire go unfulfilled. He begins to accept that hunger. He says to himself, "I want a drink right now. But so what? It's not going to happen. I can't handle a sip, so this desire is going to go unfulfilled, this thirst will go unquenched, this hunger will be unmet. Deal with it." Eventually, the wild cravings will be bent by new routines, new habits, new friends, and often a new faith. The longer they live without it, the less it seems like starving. Still, when you've been eating junk, hunger can be a good thing. For the addict, hunger is proof that he is recovering.

When the kingdom of God comes to you and you yield to it, surrendering to Jesus as the true King of the world, you are a bit like a recovering addict. You slowly realize all the destructive patterns and habits you had formed and begin to embrace a new way of living. The cravings persist, but the power of the Holy Spirit is now at work in you, helping you to resist. Eventually though, you must learn to live hungry. You must make your peace with being empty on the world. This is a good kind of *hungry*.

The trouble is it's hard to stay hungry because there is a lot to fill up on in the world. When I was younger, I thought the "things of the world" were obvious: the drugs, the drinking, the cursing, the bad movies and rock music. Those were the "evil pleasures" of the world. They were "cheap imitations," I was told.

As I got older, I realized that the real dangers of this world were not the obvious things. In fact they were pretty good things. When I say "the world," I mean "humanity organizing itself apart from God." Not the cosmos but the people, structures, cultures, habits, and practices that insist on independence from God. The world, in that sense, has plenty to offer that is sublime and deadly. There is the pride of achievement that creeps into my heart with every little success I experience. There is the delight in the praise of others that starts off innocently enough but eventually becomes a thirst that must be repeatedly quenched. There is the tiny rush that comes from seeing new books coming in the mail, or purchasing a new gadget or device. They're not evil things, not even excessive things. But gradually the creeping weed of avarice has worked its way into my heart.

There is nothing *wrong* with taking pleasure in a job well done or appreciating the praise of your peers. It is normal to get excited about getting new stuff. But drink too deeply of these things, and you get hooked. We eventually hunger for the things we feed on. We start to live for the approval of others, strive for better houses and nicer vacations, work for a status we think will satisfy us. It happens almost automatically. The steady stream of culture flows this way, its currents pulling us to achieve more, acquire more, consume more.

Years ago I heard a story of an Asian student who went abroad to get his college education. To save money, he ate instant noodles every day for every meal. He thought it was a good plan. A few years later he was dead. The acids and preservatives in his daily meals eventually got the best of him. That is what happens to us when we fill up on the stuff of this world, the possessions and comforts and status and selfish pleasures. We're getting full, we think, but the truth is we're poisoning ourselves to death in small doses. This is why Jesus said, "Woe to you who are full now, for you shall be hungry" (Luke 6:25 ESV). He was not rebuking them for having a nice meal; He was chastising them for being too easily satisfied with what will ultimately destroy them. To be full on the world is to have a bloated, malnourished soul.

Worse yet, by filling ourselves with whatever we can find in this world, we have buried a deeper hunger, one that reveals what we truly need. C. S. Lewis argued that God finds our desires not too strong but too weak. We are too easily pleased. We're like a man starving in the desert, content to stuff his mouth with the sand within his grasp when a royal banqueting table is just a few yards ahead. We need a hunger that is not so easily filled, a hunger that comes from repeatedly turning down the things that others are filling up on. This is a good kind of hungry. But to be hungry at all is uncomfortable. Maybe that's just it: To be empty on the world requires a certain willingness to not get too comfortable here.

The Bread of Life

There is another way of being hungry in the right sense.

On a Saturday night last January, my wife and I, along with our kids, were having dinner with a wonderful family from the church. We had just gotten to know them and were delighted at their gracious offer to make a meal for us in their home. After eating we sat in the living room to continue our conversation and to spend a few moments praying. It was then that my wife said we needed to go. She's hardly ever sick and never overreacts when she is; I do enough of that for the both of us. So I knew something was wrong. And so did our hosts. They kindly gave us a plastic bag in case the worst were to hit on the ride home. Holly filled the bag before we had gotten the kids in the car. The stomach flu had come with punishing force. As we walked in our house, I remember thinking how glad I was that it wasn't me. I took the girls upstairs, got them ready for bed, and came back down to see my wife lying on the couch in utter misery. I felt bad for her. I felt bad for the sweet family that had invited us over. It wasn't their food that made Holly ill. The virus had hit our kids the week before, but we thought we had survived unscathed. Not so. What a lousy way to end the weekend.

Then, without much warning, I was bent over the sink, violently expelling the contents of my digestive system. Both of us had several rounds like that, each one leaving us curled up in a lifeless ball on the couch after it was over. Thankfully the girl who rents our basement is a good friend. She and her friend ran to the store, got us Gatorade, Sprite, and lots of saltine crackers. Not only that, but she helped take care of our then two-month-old son for much of the night. By morning the worst was over. We were weak and tired, and our abdominal muscles felt like we had done a thousand crunches.

For a person who has the stomach flu or food poisoning, there's no desire to take anything in. The first aim—the only aim—is to get it out. And when you do, you finally find relief. It's one of the few times that emptiness feels good. Emptiness is actually the sign that it's over, that whatever got in you—whether from a virus or bacteria, whether from infection or intake—is now out of you. When emptiness gives way to hunger, that's usually when you know you're in the clear. It was late on Sunday afternoon when Holly and I felt our appetites return. For us, hunger was proof that we were recovering.

When you welcome the rule of God in your life, you are like a person with the stomach flu. The infection of a world that has decided to live apart from God had gotten into you. You were embroiled in a rebellion against the Creator-God. But when you say yes to God and His kingdom, He starts working inside you and begins the purge. Emptiness is only the start. Soon there will be a hunger for good food, a longing for righteousness, as Matthew put it in his gospel.

The good kind of hungry, then, can be seen in two ways. It is, as we discovered earlier, the result of refusing to fill up on what the world offers. But it is also the response of a disciple who has tasted of Jesus, the Bread of Life, and longs for more. This kind of hunger is a sign of health, an indication that the sickness in our soul is leaving and we are rising off the couch, ready for what truly nourishes.

Echoing Isaiah's prophecy of Messiah, Jesus declared, "I am the bread of life. He who comes to me will never go hungry, and he who believes in me will never be thirsty" (John 6:35). To hunger for God is to feed on Him, and feeding on Him is the end of all longing. He is where all our desires have been pointing all along. C. S. Lewis, in describing his journey from atheism to Christianity, found the strange and unfulfilled longings within the human heart to be a clue:

> If I find in myself a desire which no experience in this world can satisfy, the most probable explanation is that I was made for another world. If none of my earthly pleasures satisfy it, that does not prove that the universe is a fraud. Probably earthly pleasures were never meant to satisfy it, but only to arouse it, to suggest the real thing. If that is so, I must take care, on the one hand, never to despise, or be unthankful for, these earthly blessings, and on the other, never to mistake them for something else of which they are only a kind of a copy, or echo, or mirage.[2]

Earthly food is supposed to point us to heavenly manna. All the best of joys and the purest of pleasures we find here on earth are but a taste of what is to come. Joy here is a signpost to the eternal joy found in God. When we taste joys on earth—the joy of time with people we love, the beauty of a long walk in the mountains, the pleasure of helping a person in need—we are eating from God's table. But to taste the good and stop short of the best is like quitting after the appetizer. All that is truly good here is the "inbreaking" of God. Follow those clues and we'll find Him, "the Father of the heavenly lights" who gives "every good and perfect gift" (James 1:17).

The best and most perfect gift the Father gives us is Jesus, the Bread from heaven, who has come down and "gives life to the world" (John 6:32–33). To hunger for Him is the beginning of our awakening. It is a sign we are recovering from the infection of the world.

Give Them Something to Eat

To hunger for God is more than a longing for an experience. We often use words like *hunger* and *thirst* in our modern expressions of worship. What we often mean by that, though, is that we are longing for an emotional jolt, an experiential, music-driven euphoria on a mass scale. Even though God does frequently make His presence felt, to hunger for God is much deeper than a craving for an experience. It is to meditate on Him, on His life and His words. It is to take Him into us so that we become what we eat.

But hungering for God and His righteousness also means that we long—as He longs—to see things set right. When we embrace a hunger that comes from resisting what the world offers and feast instead on Jesus, we become more aware of those who are hungry now—in their bellies and in their souls. We begin to notice those who are dissatisfied with what they've been consuming even though they may not know why. And we notice those who *literally* need something to eat.

When Jesus heard the news of His cousin's gruesome beheading, He wanted to be alone. But the crowd that followed Him that day was hungry. Jesus had retreated by boat, attempting to find a solitary place. The crowd somehow anticipated where He was going and ran around the Sea of Galilee so quickly they beat Him there. They were hungry, hungry for something only Jesus could give them. Hungry enough to take the journey on foot. When His boat arrived at the shore and the crowd was there to greet Him with their longing eyes, Jesus didn't get back in and sail away. Their hunger stirred His compassion. Moved by their need, Jesus healed those who were sick among them.

By the time evening came, He must have been tired and hungry. At least the disciples were. They came to Jesus and suggested He dismiss the people. *Look, we're in the middle of nowhere. They were crazy enough to follow You here. But enough's enough. They got what they wanted. Send them off. Let them head to the villages and buy their own food.*

Jesus saw their spiritual longing and had compassion; the disciples saw their physical hunger and wanted to dismiss them. This was the perfect moment to teach His disciples something about the kingdom of God. *You give them something to eat,* He told them.

What? How? We have only five loaves of bread and two fish!

Give it to Me, Jesus said. He calmly seated them on the grass. Looking to heaven, Jesus blessed the food, broke it, and gave it to them. And they ate. And ate. And ate. And still, there were twelve baskets of leftovers.

Few things appear in all four gospels. The death and resurrection are in all accounts, for they are the pinnacle of what Christ came to do. His birth, on the other hand, is not in all accounts. Mark's gospel races us to the cross; John chooses the poetic "big picture" language to begin his story. The feeding of the five thousand, though, is in every gospel. There is something about this act that is significant. It is a Messiah act. As God fed the people who followed Moses in the desert with manna from heaven, Jesus fed the crowd that followed Him into a remote area. But Jesus goes further than Moses. He doesn't just bring bread from heaven; He himself is the Bread from heaven, a Bread that satisfies all hunger. Jesus said as much shortly after feeding the five thousand, which underscores the message of the miracle. This was no party trick; this was an announcement that He, Messiah, had finally come to Israel. And feeding the crowd that day was merely a foreshadowing of the feast He would one day bring to all people. Earthly bread was pointing to *heavenly Manna.* Temporary filling was a way of awakening hope for the final feast.

I think the same is true when we bring bread to the hungry. When we feed those who are empty on the world—literally and spiritually—we are helping them anticipate the fullness of who Christ is and what Christ is bringing. When we serve food to the homeless, when we invite a friend over for dinner, when we sit with our own family at dinner, it is never just a meal. It is a Messiah act, a way of pointing to the redemption and rescue that has already begun. Meals are, in a sense, sacred. This is why Jesus says to His disciples—then and now—"You give them something to eat." Every time we feed the hungry, help an addict, encourage one another to refrain from filling up on the world, lead someone to feast on Christ and His Word, we are reminding them of the luck that is now theirs, of the Feast of Messiah that is coming. We are echoing His announcement of blessing on those who are hungry now; we are telling them that they will be filled, truly filled, in the age to come.

Lucky are those who are empty on this world, for they will be filled with Jesus and feast with Him in the age to come.

DISCUSSION QUESTIONS

1. Have you gone without something that you were used to having, like sugar or caffeine or TV? Or have you ever had to unlearn a bad habit? What was that experience like?

2. What does it mean for you to be "empty on this world," to not fill up on what the world offers?

3. Hunger can be the result of going without things that are destructive, but it can also be the sign that you desire the right things. How have you seen one or both types of hunger in your life?

4. How full or comfortable or easily satisfied are you with what the world offers—whether it's sinful or not?

CHAPTER FIVE

THOSE WHOSE BEST LIFE ISN'T NOW

We had lost a pregnancy before, but this time felt different. Maybe because it had been almost three years since our last child and there was more expectancy, more excitement about being pregnant again. Maybe because the loss was prolonged and painful. Maybe because the worst of it unfolded while we were in Malaysia on a ministry trip, away from our doctor, our home, our comfort.

The plan had been to stay in Malaysia for an extra week after the conference for a vacation with my parents. We had braved the almost thirty hours of flights and layovers with our daughters, four and three at the time, and made it across the Pacific. But the joy of being back in Malaysia to teach and lead worship was muted by the gnawing loss we were experiencing. We had to get home. The vacation would have to wait for another year. When the wheels of our plane touched the runway in Denver, it had all the emotional weight of a crash landing. The relief of being home was suffocated by the heaviness of knowing that we weren't supposed to be home yet. We were supposed to be enjoying time with my parents and anticipating the birth of another child.

We returned home the week of Thanksgiving, and because we had planned to be in Malaysia that week, we found ourselves quite alone that Thursday. We made a meal—turkey, potatoes, the works— and tried to take it all in. Sitting on the couch by my wife, she melted into quiet tears. I couldn't stop them from pooling in my eyes and running over. So much hope. So much joy. So much believing for the best. Hope fills you up and makes you soar; disappointment deflates and brings you crashing down. The void is unbearable. And so we mourned.

Then in February of 2009, we were expecting again. We were thrilled. Yet the joy was tempered by the realization of how precarious the early weeks of a pregnancy are. We marked the date on the calendar for the "heartbeat appointment," the point after which miscarriages become increasingly unlikely. Since I was on a six-week sabbatical at the time, we decided it would be best if I stayed home with the girls while Holly went in for the appointment. That morning we sat in our living room and sang a few worship songs and prayed. Through tears we acknowledged that God holds us and our children in His hands ... and that we would trust His goodness no matter what. As we prayed, this simple chorus came out of my heart: "In all things, God is working ... for our good and for His glory, God is working now."

Then Holly left, and I hoped for time to move quickly. I kept looking at my cell phone to see if she had texted to say that everything was OK. I headed to my piano room with the girls and began to sing the chorus over and over. Through tears the

verse became my simple confession: "I believe in Jesus...." Then
the bridge was an eruption from my heart of faith—confidence
in who God is:

> *You are the rock we're standing on*
> *You are the love we're counting on*
> *You are the God who never fails*
> *You speak Your Word and it remains*

The notes from the piano and the strained melodies from my
voice were interrupted by a digital sound. My phone was ringing. It
was Holly. Everything was fine. We were both crying. About seven
months later, little Jonas David Packiam was born.

A Long Road of Tears

Mourning was a familiar experience for the Jews listening to Jesus.
Their story began as a people on the move, a family looking for a
Promised Land. But along the way was trouble and oppression at
every turn.

First was a king who made Abraham so afraid that he lied
about his wife being his sister. Then an uncle who tricked Jacob,
Abraham's grandson, into working much longer than he had
hoped. Then came a long stay in Egypt that saw them multiply
from a large clan to a sprawling people. Like Jacob's uncle had
done to Jacob, Egypt turned the blessing of provision for Jacob's
descendants into work they could neither choose nor escape. Israel,
legitimately now a people, went from beneficiaries of Egypt's wealth

to slaves of the Pharaohs' dreams. After their miraculous exodus, came a long, wandering walk in the wilderness that ended with a generation being buried in the sand. To enter the Promised Land, they had to fight back a fierce and hostile people. And even when they settled in the land, they remained vulnerable to invasion from larger neighboring nations.

Though our Scriptures tell Israel's story with them as the main character, from the vantage point of the larger, more-powerful nations, they were the sideshow. They were the kid at recess buried in a book on the field where older boys played football. Grass, dirt, bruises, and blows all ended up on their face. Israel's kings were tempted to make alliances with stronger nations. Egypt was an old, familiar choice. When Israel finally fractured in two kingdoms, Israel in the north and Judah in the south, it was only a matter of time before their assailants would prevail. The ten tribes of the northern kingdom fell to the Assyrians and were scattered across the region. The two tribes of the southern kingdom were taken by the Babylonians and remained in exile for at least seventy years. And even after they returned and rebuilt the walls and the temple, there were invasions from the Syrians that desecrated their holy places. A brief period of peace and independence came after the Maccabean revolt. But it ended when the Romans stretched their empire across the region.

Israel's history is the story of long stretches of wandering, exile, hardship, and oppression and brief periods of peace and prosperity. And so they mourned. But not just as a sadness about their plight. Israel believed much of their hardship—particularly all the stuff that came after they got settled in the Promised Land—was God's judgment for their repeated idolatry, syncretism, and overall failure to keep covenant with Yahweh. Mourning, in the language of the Old Testament, was the standard response of God's people to God's discipline. Isaiah, one of Israel's most powerful and poetic prophetic voices, cried out, "Jerusalem staggers, Judah is falling; their words and deeds are against the LORD, defying his glorious presence.... The gates of Zion will lament and mourn; destitute, she will sit on the ground" (Isa. 3:8, 26).

In Lamentations, the Weeper sings:

> *After affliction and harsh labor,*
> *   Judah has gone into exile.*
> *She dwells among the nations;*
> *   she finds no resting place.*
> *All who pursue her have overtaken her*
> *   in the midst of her distress.*
> *The roads to Zion mourn,*
> *   for no one comes to her appointed feasts.*
> *All her gateways are desolate,*
> *   her priests groan,*
> *her maidens grieve,*
> *   and she is in bitter anguish.*
> *Her foes have become her masters;*
> *   her enemies are at ease.*
> *The LORD has brought her grief*
> *   because of her many sins.*
> *Her children have gone into exile,*
> *   captive before the foe. (Lam. 1:3–5)*

But the strong voice of Isaiah still echoes with hope:

> *The Spirit of the Sovereign LORD is on me,*
>   *because the LORD has anointed me*
>   *to preach good news to the poor.*
> *He has sent me to bind up the brokenhearted,*
>   *to proclaim freedom for the captives*
>   *and release from darkness for the prisoners,*
> *to proclaim the year of the LORD's favor*
>   *and the day of vengeance of our God,*
> *to comfort all who mourn,*
>   *and provide for those who grieve in Zion—*
> *to bestow on them a crown of beauty*
>   *instead of ashes,*
> *the oil of gladness*
>   *instead of mourning,*
> *and a garment of praise*
>   *instead of a spirit of despair.*
> *They will be called oaks of righteousness,*
>   *a planting of the LORD*
>   *for the display of his splendor. (Isa. 61:1–3)*

The Comfort of Messiah

If the copies among the Dead Sea Scrolls of the Qumran community are any indication, the books most popular by the first century were Deuteronomy, Psalms, and Isaiah. Perhaps Deuteronomy for its clear restatement of Yahweh's covenant with Israel; Psalms for its songs and prayers that had nourished their hearts in exile; and Isaiah for its voice of hope and expectation of a coming Messiah. For various reasons, not the least of which were the popular interpretations of Isaiah's and Daniel's prophecies, the Jews of Jesus' day were particularly expectant of Messiah's arrival. They were looking for a Messiah who would end their oppression and bring comfort to the mourner. He was to come, by their calculations, any day *then*.

Then one Sabbath day, Jesus walked into a synagogue as was His custom. But this time He stood up to read. The Isaiah scroll was handed to Him. He opened it to the passage we know of as Isaiah 61. "The Spirit of the Lord is on me, because he has anointed me to preach good news to the poor ... freedom for the prisoners ... the recovery of sight for the blind ... to release the oppressed, to proclaim the year of the Lord's favor," He read (Luke 4:18–19). Before any could verbalize the question in their hearts, Jesus answered it by simply saying, "Today this scripture is fulfilled in your hearing" (4:21).

Two chapters later, when Jesus announced, "You're blessed when the tears flow freely. Joy comes with the morning" (6:21 MSG), He was declaring again that the long-awaited Messiah had indeed come. They had mourned in sorrow at God's discipline for a long time, but now the hope of restoration was on the horizon. Comfort had arrived.

If Israel's mourning was an act of repentance that God was now meeting with restoration, comfort, and hope, then it is fair to suggest that the mourning that Jesus is calling *blessed* is the kind of mourning that is a godly sorrow, a deep remorse and repentance for sin. Much has been written on this Beatitude to draw out an admonishment toward repentance, and it is certainly valuable and true.

But there is another aspect of mourning and comfort. When the New Testament writers speak of comfort, they also talk of comfort that comes in the midst of a suffering that is unrelated to God's discipline. There was a species of trouble the first Christians knew that was not because of any *unfaithfulness* to God but resulted instead from their *faithfulness* to Messiah. The first Christians went so far as to see their suffering for Christ to be a sort of sharing in Christ's suffering. And because they were sharing in Messiah's suffering they would also share in His comfort. Paul said it this way: "Praise be to the God and Father of our Lord Jesus Christ, the Father of compassion and the God of all comfort, who comforts us in all our troubles, so that we can comfort those in any trouble with the comfort we ourselves have received from God. For just as the sufferings of Christ flow over into our lives, so also through Christ our comfort overflows" (2 Cor. 1:3–5).

When Jesus said, "Lucky are those who mourn," He was neither mocking their sorrow nor applauding their repentance. He was announcing the arrival of God's comfort. Jesus' listeners were not blessed first for their mourning but for the comfort that was coming, the comfort that He Himself was bringing.

God in the Garden of Good and Evil

To mourn is to protest. It is to say that this should not be.

We mourn when we lose a friend in a car accident. We mourn when we lose a child in pregnancy. We mourn when an earthquake collapses buildings upon untold hundreds of lives we never knew. We mourn when a husband walks out on his wife and children. We mourn when a son turns away from his mother and father. We mourn when an economy that enables greed leads powerful people to exploit the powerless. We mourn when disease destroys a life in its prime, when an addiction takes down a life that had so much promise. These and more are occasions when we mourn, when we protest, when from the depths of our souls we cry out, "This is not supposed to happen!"

And we're right. To mourn is to protest. And to protest is to give witness to a better reality. It is a sign in our souls that we are in on God's secret: All is not as God intends. This isn't quite the world God made. All is not the way it should be. Sin is at work. Evil has infected the cosmos. Just as Israel was kicked out of the Promised Land because of their rebellion against Yahweh, the whole universe is in exile because of humanity's rebellion against Creator-God in the garden.[1] And as Israel mourned, so the whole world mourns, lamenting the brokenness. In mourning we protest the infection of evil, crying out that this is not how it should be. Perhaps there is a faint memory of Eden in our hearts. We have been wandering in exile for so long it's hard to know.

We can see and taste and feel the evidence of a good creation infected by evil. But what of God? What does He think? Here things take a surprising twist. God is not watching from a distance, waiting to make the earth dissolve like snow and start over. By this point in our journey together in this book, we know better. We know that God, right from the garden of Eden, began looking for Adam after his rebellion. God in the garden was working within His newly fallen creation. God in the garden. God the Gardener.

Then in the fullness of time, God became flesh. Jesus entered our suffering, joined in our mourning, and continued working from within His fallen creation. One of the stories He told was of a tree that had yet to bear fruit and was about to be cut down. But the gardener told the master not to cut it down yet. "Let me surround it with manure and work with it for another year," the gardener said (see Luke 13:6–9). Always patient. Always working. God the Gardener.

Toward the end of Jesus' time on earth, God was in a garden again, agonizingly at work within His fallen creation. Jesus, praying, surrendering, blood dripping from His forehead under the weight of what He was about to do. Jesus, at the cross, took the full weight of evil on Himself. He drank the poison that had infected the universe. Like in the scene from *The Count of Monte Cristo*, it was as if, on the cross, Jesus said, "Do your worst, and when you are done, I will do mine." And He did. He rose from the grave, conquering death and hell, signifying that death would not reign forever. Jesus was more than Messiah who brought comfort to a mourning Israel, suffering in prolonged exile. He was the one who rescued all creation from exile. By rising from the grave, Jesus announced to the world that it would not always be this way. As Paul explained to the Corinthian church, because Christ has been raised from the dead, "He is the first of a great harvest of all who have died" (1 Cor. 15:20 NLT). God in the garden sowed the seed of His life for a harvest of new creation.

Shortly after Jesus had risen, Mary Magdalene wept at the empty tomb, thinking His body had been taken away. Jesus stood before her, but she mistook Him for a gardener (John 20:15). Not a bad mistake. The Gardener is at work in His garden, and the garden itself longs for the work to be complete:

> *For all creation is waiting eagerly for that future day when God will reveal who his children really are. Against its will, all creation was subjected to God's curse. But with eager hope, the creation looks forward to the day when it will join God's children in glorious freedom from death and decay. For we know that all creation has been groaning as in the pains of childbirth right up to the present time.* (Rom. 8:19–22 NLT)

By taking the full weight of humanity's rebellion and the full force of evil, Jesus entered our mourning and defeated evil at its root. He sowed His life and rose again as the firstfruits of a coming harvest, a day when heaven and earth will be made new. The cross was a decisive moment of victory over evil; the resurrection a sign of what is to come. God the Gardener is at work within the garden of His fallen creation, working to rescue and redeem.

Hope

But sometimes all we see is manure.

We see the bombs in train stations, the car wrecks that cut down youth in bloom, the earthquakes that decimate cities. We see the men and women who live to ruin others, the ones who are set on causing destruction. We see the greed in our own hearts, the lust, the pride, the insatiable thirst to get more, be more, do more. As Aleksandr Solzhenitsyn wrote, the "line separating good and evil passes not through states, nor between classes, nor between political parties either—but right through every human heart—and through all human hearts."[2]

What do we do with all the suffering in the world? For one, we mourn. And in our mourning, we remember that Jesus wept. Jesus, God, entered our world of suffering. He understands what it feels like to work with sweat on His brow. He knows the pain of betrayal by a friend. He has suffered the rejection and mocking abuse by people that should have loved Him—indeed, by people who once did. He experienced the death of a dear friend. When He saw Mary and the others weeping over Lazarus' death, He was "deeply moved in spirit and troubled" (John 11:33). The word John uses there indicates a deep groaning, a gut-level grunt of grief.

Up until this point, Jesus had been telling Martha about the resurrection. She keeps trying to convey the shock of Lazarus' death; He keeps speaking mysteriously about *being* the resurrection. It is when He sees Mary and the others with her crying that He weeps. He sees their tears and shares their sorrow deep in His gut. Then when they show Him where they have placed the body, He weeps. This is important to know: that we are not alone in grief, that when we see trouble, evil bearing fruit in death, we mourn and God mourns with us. A soul-baring, bone-deep agony of protest against the wrong that has occurred.

But God does more than join us in our suffering. God works with the manure. He takes the refuse and makes it fertilizer. From deep within our mess, God is bringing life. To say it again: On the cross Jesus took the full weight of evil and suffering and pain and brokenness and sin and triumphed over it. In His resurrection we know that new creation has begun: God will "do for the cosmos what

He has done for Jesus."[3] Life is springing up from the pile of dirt and dung. There will be resurrection.

And that is reason for hope, for confidence, for comfort. In the earlier passage where Paul, writing to the Corinthians, said that "just as the sufferings of Christ flow over into our lives, so also through Christ our comfort overflows" (2 Cor. 1:5), he explains the source of this comfort in the verses that follow:

> *We do not want you to be uninformed, brothers, about the hardships we suffered in the province of Asia. We were under great pressure, far beyond our ability to endure, so that we despaired even of life. Indeed, in our hearts we felt the sentence of death. But this happened that we might not rely on ourselves but on God, who raises the dead. (2 Cor. 1:8–9)*

They were experiencing real hardship. They despaired to the point of thinking that they would lose their lives. Death was imminent, impending, seemingly inevitable. And yet in the midst of that, they learned to rely on "God, who raises the dead."

What kind of hope do we have? Is it that one day we'll fly away? Is it that God is a distant designer who feels somewhat apologetic about all the suffering in the world He made? Is God's way to watch from afar and say, "Whoops. That's too bad. Well, there's a floating paradise you'll one day enter and so … there." Certainly not. Our hope is rooted in the belief that God is at work now, from within His fallen creation, to rescue and redeem it and to one day remake it. And that in Jesus' life, death, and resurrection, He has indeed done it. He has taken on evil and triumphed over it. The victory that began at Calvary will culminate in Christ's return. How do we know this? The resurrection of Jesus gives us solid grounds for that hope. Because Jesus was raised from the dead with a new life and a new resurrected body (unlike Lazarus, who was raised from the dead only to die again), we are learning to rely on the "God who raises the dead." What this means is that trouble, suffering, pain is temporary but God's comfort—the hope of resurrection!—is final. Our mourning is for the moment; our comfort is forever.

Isaiah caught a glimpse of this when he wrote:

> *He will swallow up death forever.*
> *The Sovereign* LORD *will wipe away the tears*
>   *from all faces;*
> *he will remove the disgrace of his people*
>   *from all the earth.*
>   *The* LORD *has spoken. (Isa. 25:8)*

Tears will be wiped away because death—the worst that evil could do—will be swallowed up. Paul sees this as being fulfilled in Jesus. Using the prophet's exact words, Paul reminds us of the hope that we have because Jesus has risen from the grave. Christ's victory over death means that we will have victory over death. We will gain new, resurrected bodies, and when we do, we can say, "Death has been swallowed up in victory" (1 Cor. 15:54). It has no sting (v. 55).

Isaiah also saw a day when God would make everything new:

> *"Behold, I will create*
>   *new heavens and a new earth.*

The former things will not be remembered,
*   nor will they come to mind.*
But be glad and rejoice forever
*   in what I will create,*
for I will create Jerusalem to be a delight
*   and its people a joy.*
I will rejoice over Jerusalem
*   and take delight in my people;*
the sound of weeping and of crying
*   will be heard in it no more." (Isa. 65:17–19)*

Hundreds of years later, when the first Christians were suffering at the hands of the Romans, John, marooned on the island of Patmos, saw the day when Isaiah's vision would come fully to pass:

Then I saw a new heaven and a new earth, for the first heaven and the first earth had passed away, and there was no longer any sea. I saw the Holy City, the new Jerusalem, coming down out of heaven from God, prepared as a bride beautifully dressed for her husband. And I heard a loud voice from the throne saying, "Now the dwelling of God is with men, and he will live with them. They will be his people, and God himself will be with them and be their God. He will wipe every tear from their eyes. There will be no more death or mourning or crying or pain, for the old order of things has passed away." (Rev. 21:1–4)

Life Is Breaking Through

But what of the in-between, the moments between Isaiah's vision and John's revelation of what happens in the end? Paul says that, because of Jesus, new creation has, in fact, begun. "If anyone is in Christ," Paul wrote, "he is a new creation; the old has gone, the new has come!" (2 Cor. 5:17).

We are in the final bars of the song; the ending overture has begun. People nowadays say we are living in the last days, but what they usually mean is that the world is awful, and the Devil is at work. What the first Christians believed is that, because we are living in the last days, the end of the age, new creation has begun! Victory has started to unfold. Comfort is coming. Indeed it has come.

Imagine that a man takes you to a junkyard covered with rusted metal and decomposing parts, littered with paper bags and used up cups. Imagine that he tells you that this very ground will be a beautiful garden.

"No way," you say. "This place is covered with trash and refuse. This is a junkyard, not a garden."

"True," the man says. "It is a junkyard now. But I just bought it and will make it a garden. In fact, I've already started my work."

"What?" you say. "It looks the same as it did last week. How is anything different?"

The man gently replies, "I have already planted some flowers."

"Where?" you ask. "I don't see anything."

But its work is beneath the soil. Suddenly he points to a green shoot breaking through the earth. "Look! There it is. I planted that recently. There is a small sign of what is coming."

This is a bit like what Christ has done. He has taken this world, a good creation gone bad, rotting and decomposing, and redeemed it. And He will one day make all things new. How do we know this? How do we know that a new creation is coming?

"Look," Christ says, pointing to your heart. "New creation has already begun. It is springing up in you, and in everyone who has given his life over to Me." The green shoots breaking through the dirt in your heart are evidence of God's redemptive, re-creating work in the whole cosmos.

This is what Jesus was getting at when He said, "Blessed are you who weep now, for you will laugh" (Luke 6:21). You are blessed not for your mourning, but for the comfort that is coming. You are not lucky for your tears but for the laughter that is coming.

So. In a world of suffering and pain, we mourn. But in the midst of our mourning, we realize that God mourns with us, and we remember that Jesus has triumphed over evil and so death will one day end. Moreover we carry this hope to others who mourn. We "comfort those in any trouble with the comfort we ourselves have received from God" (2 Cor. 1:4). Jesus the Messiah carries a comfort deeper than anything we have ever known. We who were mourning are lucky, for this comfort has come to us. Now we who have received this comfort carry it to those who mourn.

Carriers of Comfort

Six bags.

Six bags were all they had to fit their life in. They were leaving in the morning for Cambodia, and Jacob and Noelle had to make some difficult decisions about what to take with them and what to leave behind. The most difficult decision, though, had been made over a year ago when they decided they were going to move to Cambodia. But the truth is the journey began years before even that.

Noelle had been going on short-term mission trips since she was fourteen but had always been glad to return to America. But in 2005, in her mid-twenties, she took a trip to Nepal with theMILL, New Life Church's college/twentysomething ministry, and everything began to change. *I could live overseas*, she thought to herself. Still she returned, took a job as pastoral counselor to the young women in theMILL, and wondered when the day would come.

Jacob, in a similar way, had developed a heart for ministry overseas through several short-term trips but never envisioned himself living anywhere but America. *I could support missionaries,* he thought. *I'll have a big house and provide a haven for missionaries on furlough.* As the IT manager for Compassion International, Jacob was content to facilitate someone else's work overseas. But the more trips he took with theMILL, particularly in the summers of '05 and '06, the more he began to consider actually *becoming* a missionary.

When Jacob and Noelle started an unlikely dating relationship, neither spoke initially of their desire to do ministry overseas. At times it might even have seemed that they had different visions of their future. Yet quietly the burden for long-term mission work— particularly in Asia—began to grow in each of them. In the spring of 2007, they had dinner with Eric and Ginny Hanson, the directors of an international ministry called In His Steps International and founders of In His Steps Cambodia (www.ihsionline.org), which I mentioned in chapter 3. Eric and Ginny had come to the States on furlough, and since Noelle was leading a team from theMILL to Cambodia that summer and would be working with their ministry, it was a chance to connect. They had no idea the seeds that would be planted in their hearts that night. They learned that Eric and Ginny had started In His Steps International in 2004 and launched In His Steps Cambodia as a local NGO that would train and empower locals to reach other locals with the gospel. Through daily English classes for hundreds of children, weekend youth and children's programs, and a church plant, they are beginning to rescue and redeem Cambodia from the desolation of a wicked past dictator and the present horrors of human trafficking. One of the most beautiful things In His Steps Cambodia does is a ministry called Sak Saum, which I also mentioned earlier. Sak Saum is a ministry to vulnerable and exploited women, women who have escaped or been rescued from human trafficking. Through Sak Saum they receive counseling, education, training in job skills, health care, and ongoing discipleship. As Jacob and Noelle listened to Eric and Ginny that night in the spring of 2007, something was coming alive inside them.

That summer, while Jacob led a team of Air Force cadets to Thailand and Noelle led a team to Cambodia, their burden for Asia began to grow. While Noelle was in Cambodia, sitting in a devotional time with Cambodian girls, listening to them pray in Khmer, it became clear that she would live there someday. One piece of the picture was coming into focus. The other pieces were soon to follow. It also became clear that their futures belonged together. And so, on January 6, 2008, Jacob and Noelle laid all their hopes and fears at the feet of Christ and covenanted their lives to each other in marriage. A year later they took a brief scouting trip to Cambodia to confirm their decision. It was settled. Jacob and Noelle announced their plan to move to Cambodia. By the opening weeks of March 2010, it was time to decide what to put in the six bags they were taking with them.

When they got to Cambodia, they met a woman named Theavy. Theavy's story is heavy. Trafficked twice as a young girl, she somehow managed to escape both times, though not without deep damage to her fragile heart. "Fear, a low self-worth, and a deep hunger to be loved and safe" is how Noelle described the condition of Theavy's heart. Theavy eventually got married and looked forward to the day when she would have her own child, a child to nurture and love the way she had longed to be loved. It took nine years for that day to come. And when it miraculously did, she named her son *Sokun,* which means "a gift from God." Rather than marking the end of her troubles, the birth of their son somehow triggered something destructive in Theavy's husband. Shortly after Sokun's birth, Theavy discovered that her husband was in debt-bondage to prostitutes. He then abandoned them and went off to pursue a different life.

But because of Eric and Ginny Hanson, Theavy was not alone. Just as they had helped Theavy through earlier struggles, they were there for her in her abandonment. Ginny walked with Theavy in her grief, providing love and counsel and comfort. Hope began to flicker in the darkness. When Jacob and Noelle met Theavy, she had just become the new national director of Sak Saum and of In His Steps Cambodia. She is now giving her life to help other girls find the same hope and healing that she did more than five years ago.

It's easy to see Theavy's story replaying in the young girls that are now helped through Sak Saum. They are fragile and damaged and afraid. But comfort has come. Hope has already begun. As Jacob and Noelle sit and pray and counsel and walk with the girls in Sak Saum and the orphans and children in the Foundation Center and SafeHouse in Saang, they can't help but think of the redemption that Jesus is bringing to them, a rescue that they are carrying to them. What Ginny did for Theavy, they are doing for these little ones. Jacob and Noelle are bringing comfort to those who mourn, making the mourners lucky for the comfort that is now theirs.

But Jacob and Noelle are carrying a comfort they themselves have received. You see, a little over ten years ago, Noelle's mother died of cancer. Two years before leaving for Cambodia, Jacob's stepmom was tragically killed in a horse-riding accident. They have both tasted bitter grief. And while there are no answers or easy solutions, they have found a comfort that is deep and eternal, one that rests on the fact that Jesus has risen from the grave. Death itself will be swallowed up in victory. Death is not the last word. The final stanza of the song is one of new life, new heaven, new earth. And it has already begun. There is a minor-key motif in this ending movement, but it breaks into a triumphant strain in the final bars. The comfort that Jacob and Noelle have tasted and the comfort they carry is the hope—rooted in Christ's resurrection—that what's coming, what has already begun to come, is better than what is and even what was.

Lucky are those whose best life is not now, for what is coming is better than what is.

DISCUSSION QUESTIONS

1. How is mourning like protesting?

2. Have you ever protested a particular reality, wishing it wasn't true, crying out that it is not supposed to be this way?

3. How does it help to imagine Jesus joining us in our protest, to know that He agrees that all is not the way it should be, that this is not how God made His world to be?

4. How does the vision of resurrection and the final restoration of all things as discussed in this chapter reshape your picture of comfort and hope?

CHAPTER SIX

THOSE WHOM THE WORLD REJECTS

The church was only a few months old when they decided to find a way to reach out to their community.

My parents, along with a handful of others, started the church—uniquely named The Dwelling Place—in a remote, developing township about an hour outside Kuala Lumpur, the capital city of Malaysia. The first congregants, besides my sister and I, were a handful of immigrant workers who had been brought in to help with the many new construction projects.

Bukit Beruntung, the name of the developing township, was the vision of several corporate developers partnering to create a large planned community of sorts that would take a few decades to fully unfold. When we moved there in September 1995, the township project was only a year or so old. But Bukit Beruntung hadn't been a large vacant parcel of land. It had been occupied by several poor squatter communities. When the developers moved in, they built low-cost apartments and helped relocate many families there. Just outside the developing township was a small town called Rawang, also with many low-income families. Many of these low-income families, from both Bukit Beruntung and Rawang, happen to be of Indian descent and speak almost no English. Tamil, an Indian dialect, is their mother tongue. Many of the children from these families attend a Tamil-language public school in the area. It was to the children of that school that The Dwelling Place planned its first outreach.

It was Christmas season, and though there is little in the weather of a Malaysian December to invoke holiday mirth, Malaysians do their best to celebrate the season. Whether it's from Bing Crosby Christmas movies or vestiges of being a British colony or simply a fascination with all things European-American, Malaysians are will-ing to indulge romanticized feelings for the Christmas season even if they are from other religions. So when my parents invited the children from the Tamil-language school to come for a Christmas play, their families must have thought it was innocent enough. That Christmas evening in 1995, the children came. The Christmas play was put on by the Indonesian immigrant construction workers, who by then had become our core congregation. The children loved it. Deciding to strike while the proverbial iron was hot, my parents asked if they would be interested in English classes. They responded with eagerness. By February of the following year, English classes with children from the Tamil school became part of the church's weekly routine.

The more the people of the church got to know these children, the better they understood their need. The children came from poor homes, homes too poor to afford many basic provisions.

My parents and a few others decided to pitch in every month to provide rice, sugar, milk, and other supplies for their families. My dad would drive to their different homes, delivering these goodies like a plainclothes Santa Claus, making Christmas come once a month. Saturday English classes led to Sunday evening services, complete with Bible stories, prayer, and songs in Tamil—led in noble fashion by a non-Tamil-speaking Chinese couple who were among the church's earliest leaders. Everything was rolling. God was reaching these children and blessing their families. The people of The Dwelling Place were being luck-bearers to the least of these. The kingdom of God was breaking in.

And then things began to turn. The principal of the Tamil school, a Hindu, began to single out the children who were going to church. He refused to let them have any of the fresh milk—a special commodity in Malaysia—that the government provided for the school's students. As if that weren't enough, he told the children that if they kept going to church and accepting these gifts from the church, he would call the police, and they would come, along with the military, to arrest them. These threats were as empty as an aged coconut, but the children didn't know that. They were too young to know the ins and outs of their religious freedom, too clueless and afraid to know that they had done nothing illegal or criminal. All they knew was that an older Hindu man, a man respected in their community, was angry at them for going to church, and that he said they could go to jail.

When my father heard what the principal had been doing, he told the children to tell their parents about it, since the man had no authority to actually do what he had threatened. Things got better, but relations between the families whose children went to church for English classes and Bible stories and those who refused for reasons of their own devotion to Hinduism were strained at best.

Tempers flared again in the late months of 1997. The church was hosting a special night for the children with a guest missionary who had spent the last few decades working with children all over Asia and Eastern Europe. (As an aside, when I was a young eight-year-old in Malaysia, this very missionary spoke at a children's camp where I first sensed the Lord calling me to surrender my life. I have told that story elsewhere, in my first book, *Butterfly in Brazil*.) As the night was winding down, there was a knock at the door of the church. A couple of Indian men had come in a drunken state, angry about why children from their communities were in a church. A string of Tamil threats in raised voices broke the humid night air. My dad simply asked what was so harmful about teaching them English and helping them gain good values? They had no response. He then asked them if they were doing anything to take care of the poor in their own communities. Again no response. So why stop these families from receiving rice and milk and flour and educational help if they weren't going to do anything to help them? They muttered and shook their heads as they staggered off in the night.

The Tamil children's ministry kept growing despite these challenges. After a few years, my dad felt that the best thing for the growth of that ministry and outreach was to turn it over to a young Indian pastor in the area who led a small Tamil-language congregation. More than a decade later, that Tamil-language church is healthy and continuing to make inroads to the Indian community through an ongoing partnership with my parents' church.

The Tamil church still seems to pose a threat to the Hindu Indians. There have been angry men who have vowed to close down the church. In February 2010, the Tamil church was vandalized. The electrical wiring was stripped, and musical instruments were stolen along with sound equipment and air conditioners. The church building was inoperable for a few months. But support from other churches in the community helped the church get back on her feet, and the ministry goes on, much to the dismay of uneasy Hindus nearby. For the young Indian pastor and his growing Tamil congregation, such opposition is a good sign. The threats, the opposition, the attacks all are signs, after all, that the church is making its mark.

Lucky Rejects?

The Jews of Jesus' day were quite familiar with opposition and oppression. Outright persecution was still in their recent memory. In 168 BC, the Syrian ruler Antiochus Epiphanes IV made an attempt to homogenize the religion and culture of his empire, which included the land of Israel. When Antiochus arrived in Jerusalem, he vandalized the temple, set up an idol on the holy altar, and further desecrated it by spraying the blood of a swine— a notoriously unclean animal to the Jews—on it. But Antiochus did more than desecrate the temple. He outlawed the study of the Torah, the observance of the Sabbath, and the circumcision of Jewish boys, making those classically Jewish acts punishable by death. He was trying to erase their cultural identity. Syrian soldiers then demanded that Mattathias, a member of the Jewish priestly class, set an example to his people by sacrificing a pig on a portable pagan altar. When Mattathias refused, another Jew, eager to please or desperate to survive, volunteered. Mattathias, angered by the Syrian request and the Jewish turncoat, killed both Antiochus' representative and the Jew who had volunteered to do it.

Mattathias and his five sons fled to the Judean wilderness, hiding in the many caves and hills. A motley militia of farmers began to assemble. Like the American Minutemen against the Redcoats roughly two thousand years later, the Maccabees used guerilla warfare tactics against the powerful, well-trained Syrian army. Eventually they made their way back to the temple, reclaiming it, cleansing it, and constructing a new, undefiled altar. Exactly three years to the day after Antiochus' desecrating rampage, the Maccabees dedicated the temple with proper sacrifices and the rekindling of the menorah—the golden lamp stand—over an eight-day celebration.

That is the story of Hanukkah. And it was fresh on the Jewish minds of Jesus' audience. They knew what it was like to live under oppression. Only a few generations earlier, their people had fought to overthrow the wicked and defiling persecution of the Syrians.

So why would Jesus call the persecuted blessed? Blessed are the ones who overthrow the oppressor, not the ones who endure persecution! When Jesus announced blessing on the persecuted, it may have been the most startling part of His sermon. He had saved the most stunning bits for the end. It was as if He had been ramping up to this moment, and now that He'd gotten to this part, He repeated it, like a singer who's reached the end of the song and is vamping the last line for emphasis.

Jesus uses a popular Hebrew poetic device, parallelism, using a string of similar phrases that each adds a slightly different shade on the same core idea.

> *"Blessed are you when men hate you,*
>   *when they exclude you and insult you*
>   *and reject your name as evil,*
>   *because of the Son of Man.*

> *"Rejoice in that day and leap for joy, because great is your reward in heaven. For that is how their fathers treated the prophets." (Luke 6:22–23)*

This seems to follow what scholars of Hebrew poetry have called repetitive parallelism, where two or three—or even four!—lines repeat the idea, and the last line is a sort of "changeup." Think of a boxer coming with a right hook (POP!), another right hook (POP!), and then a surprising left uppercut (JAB!). Just as the last changeup hit is the critical blow, so the last line in a repetitive parallel sequence is where the emphasis lands.

Let's look at it section by section, or stanza by stanza. In the first stanza, Jesus is announcing blessing on those who are hated, excluded, insulted, and rejected *because* of their association with the Son of Man. Persecution is not a virtue in itself. Being a martyr for a cause is admirable, but it is not enough to be counted blessed. If the hate and the rejection are coming because of your allegiance to Jesus, however, then you're lucky.

Why?

The second stanza answers this: You are blessed *because* your reward is great in heaven. When you, because of your allegiance to Jesus, are rejected by the world, by the people and systems and structures of human rebellion against God, you have a share in a heavenly reward. And for that you are blessed. You have a part in God's future, the world set right. You have, in Matthew's parallel passage, been "persecuted because of righteousness" and so the "kingdom of heaven" is yours (Matt. 5:10). You will enjoy God's rule fully expressed: the day when nations will be humbled, kings will bow, war will cease, and justice will reign.

And then the climactic line: You—persecuted, downtrodden you!—are in the company of the great prophets of old. You, when you are persecuted for Christ's sake, are blessed not only for your share in the reward of the kingdom, but you are included among the martyrs. And it is the martyrs, as John saw in his Revelation, who will reign with Christ as He sets the world right.

You have a share in all this because you were rejected by the world. And the world's rejection of you is proof that only the place where God's will is fully done—heaven, for shorthand—is your home.

Threatened by Christians

When we read words like this, a blessing on those who are persecuted for Jesus' sake, it's hard to know what to think. Most of my readers have never really experienced any kind of persecution. Sure, we may endure a bit of scorn from journalists in the media, and yes, a neighbor may not be as warm when they discover that you go to church every Sunday. But *real* persecution, like the kind the early

Christians faced—being thrown in an arena with wild animals—or like the kind that Christians in other parts of the world face—having bags put over their heads and knives held to their throats.... We know nothing of that sort of persecution.

So we're left with a few choices. We can try to equate the church's marginalized place in society with the outright persecution that takes place in so many parts of the world. But doing that not only cheapens the suffering of the martyrs, it encourages comfortable Christians to have a pity party. Again what most of us experience is nothing near what suffering Christ-followers in darker regions of the world endure. The other option is to conclude that these blessings only apply to those special believers who courageously endure persecution on a near-daily basis. We can certainly trust that those martyrs will be greatly rewarded in heaven. But that would mean that the very last Beatitude has nothing to say to many Christians today. I'm OK with that. I'm not the sort of person who thinks everything in the Bible ought to apply to me. The Bible is a massive story within which we find meaning for our own stories, but not every detail needs to say something to *me*.

Both approaches have a measure of validity, and yet both miss a larger idea that Jesus may have been seeking to communicate: If you're being persecuted by those who have chosen to live independently of God as revealed in Jesus, it means you pose some sort of threat to their system or structure or norm. I'll show you what I mean.

I had never connected the dots before. But one afternoon, as I sat with a few guys for our Bible study on Ephesians, the pieces began to fall in place.

I knew that the early Christians weren't persecuted because Rome was somehow trying to control religion, as if it were a sort of secular regime like communist China. No, ancient Rome was happy to have a potpourri of religions indiscriminately bleeding on one another. In fact early Christians were the ones who were considered atheists because of their belief in an unseen God. There's a wonderful story about Polycarp, the bishop of Smyrna, who, as he's being led to his death, is ordered to point to his fellow Christian brothers and sisters and say, "Out with the atheists!" as a kind of denouncement of his faith. Instead Polycarp points his bony old finger at the crowd of angry and sadistic polytheistic pagans and cries, "Out with the *atheists!*"

I remember studying about the famous letter from Pliny, the Roman governor, to the emperor Trajan asking how he should handle this new sect of people, the Christians. The letter is from the early second century and has helped us understand how the Romans viewed Christians. Trajan basically told Pliny not to waste the resources of the empire seeking Christians out. Yes, their religion was technically banned, but the mere belief in Jesus was not a serious enough crime.

So why the persecutions? Because the early Christians didn't view their faith in Christ as a privately held belief. They saw it as something that had serious ramifications for the world in which they lived. They refused to hail Caesar as *kyrios* and *soter*, lord and savior. They, instead, used those very words for Jesus, affirming and announcing Him as the true Lord and Savior of the world. Paul encouraged masters to remember that they were on level ground with their slaves before Christ, and even asked Philemon to take his runaway slave, Onesimus, home as a brother. These may seem like small moves by our modern standards of freedom. But against the backdrop of a Roman society that took it for granted that some people were better than others and that the powerful had a right to push the weak around, Paul's words and actions were dramatic and stunning. The early Christians believed that the real King of the world had arrived—His name is Jesus—and He should be obeyed as such. All this was unsettling to the Roman authorities. In Acts, Paul, Silas, and their host-accomplice, Jason, were brought before the city council with the charge that they were "all guilty of treason against Caesar, for they profess allegiance to another king, named Jesus" (Acts 17:7 NLT).

Trajan's reply to Pliny in the early part of the second century affirms the scenario that Acts describes. Trajan's biggest concern with the early Christians was that they would unsettle the peace they had fought to gain within the empire. That's why, when a Christian was arrested, as a part of his trial, he would have to curse or renounce Christ and swear allegiance to the emperor. They wanted to ensure that, regardless of what a person's religion was, he would be loyal above all to Rome. There were, of course, many Christians who simply would not do that. Their refusal then gave Roman courts grounds for brutal punishment. They could now accuse Christians of undermining Rome's authority, of being a threat to empire security, and could punish them as treasonous criminals.

But the first Christians were not afraid of death. Their courage came from the fact that "God had raised Jesus from the dead"—a theme in nearly every New Testament sermon. If Jesus, who Himself had been killed at the hand of the Romans, had been raised from the dead, they knew that the Creator-God was beginning to fulfill His promise at last: that God would set everything right one day and make everything new. Since Jesus had been raised from the dead and given a new glorified body, they would one day be raised from the dead and given glorified bodies. Jews during the Maccabean period had had a similar confidence. When torturers would cut off their fingers, they would laugh and egg them on, saying that Yahweh would give them new bodies when the resurrection occurred. They echoed Job's declaration in the face of physical suffering:

> *"Oh, that my words were recorded,*
> *   that they were written on a scroll,*
> *that they were inscribed with an iron tool on lead,*
> *   or engraved in rock forever!*
> *I know that my Redeemer lives,*
> *   and that in the end he will stand upon the earth.*
> *And after my skin has been destroyed,*
> *   yet in my flesh I will see God." (Job 19:23–26)*

For the first Christians, the bodily resurrection was now a certainty, for Jesus Himself had been raised from the dead, the first among many. With no fear of death, the Romans had no leverage to keep Christians from their subversive, countercultural influence. Despite the public persecutions and gruesome torture—and maybe *because of them*—the gospel of Jesus as King of the world kept spreading throughout the empire.

Most of this I knew. But I never connected it to Paul's words in Ephesians 3:13 telling the Ephesian church, people he knew well and loved dearly, not to be discouraged about his sufferings in prison because it was their *glory*. As we sat in our Bible study on Ephesians, someone read the question out loud from the workbook: Why did Paul say that his sufferings were their glory? We sat there a little confused. We weren't quite sure.

Fortunately the workbook had a paragraph explaining the question. Paul had just said, in Ephesians 3:10, that God's intent was that "through the church, the manifold wisdom of God should be made known to the rulers and authorities in the heavenly realms." The church would reveal God's wisdom in a way that confronted spiritual rulers and authorities. Paul had earlier written, in Ephesians 2:1–2, that those who are disobedient are following the pattern of "this world and of the ruler of the kingdom of the air," allowing that spirit to work in them. In other words, there is another kingdom at work in this world. It is one of evil and darkness. And just as God's people are carriers of God's kingdom, people who insist on living in rebellion to God are participating in the dark kingdom, following the patterns of the world, carrying off an evil invasion. The church, God's people, are to live in a way that is so different that it confronts the dark kingdom, its rulers, and the people through whom that kingdom has its way. In short the people of God—just by living as the people of God here in this world—pose a sort of threat to human systems and structures of evil and oppression.

Of course Paul is not talking about being obnoxious or physically threatening evil systems. Later in the Ephesian letter, he reminds us that our battle is not with flesh and blood but with spiritual rulers (Eph. 6:12). He also writes elsewhere that Christians are to do whatever is possible to "live at peace with everyone" (Rom. 12:18). It is doubtful that Paul would have advocated belligerent picketing or angry demonstrations. What he is saying, though, is that the church, by being a loving, unified collection of diverse people, will stand in stark contrast and in opposition to the selfish, oppressive, depersonalizing systems of the world.

The fact that Paul was suffering meant that the church was really doing it: They were unnerving an oppressive empire. Paul's suffering was something they could glory in as a sign of just how subversive Christ and His kingdom truly are. Paul, the Ephesian church, and all believers everywhere are together part of God's glorious people, living against the grain of the world and its systems and ways. His suffering reminds them of it. "Don't let my present trouble on your behalf get you down," Paul wrote. "Be proud!" (Eph. 3:13 MSG).

Farm Culture

You wouldn't think a farmer would pose a threat to a powerful government.

Yet that's exactly how Joel Salatin sees himself, as a threat to U.S. government officials. Salatin runs a "family owned, multi-generational, pasture-based, beyond organic, local-market"[1] 550-acre farm in Virginia. He is prominently featured in Michael Pollan's landmark work *The Omnivore's Dilemma*, a book that explains how consumer demands over the last forty years have changed the food industry.

This "food revolution" has given rise to big-box food stores and led to the demise of the local grocer. Small farms have been swallowed up by large corporations that could produce and package large numbers of chickens and cattle. Now, whether you eat fast food or not, most of our meat comes from the same few places.

But in order to get that much beef and chicken to big-box stores and food chains, the way cows and chickens are raised had to be changed. There is no time to wait for a chicken to grow into its full stature; it needs to be genetically modified to grow faster. Cattle can't freely graze on grass. That's far too costly and time-consuming. It's much more efficient to pen them up in crowded feedlots with manure rising up to their hindquarters while they are fed corn.

Turns out there are downsides to such methods. When a cow eats grass, its digestive system naturally sheds most of the harmful bacteria it acquires. When a cow eats corn, the odds of retaining harmful bacteria skyrocket. The feedlots' solution? Inject them pre-emptively with antibiotics. Chickens are collapsing under the weight of artificially enlarged bodies that their bones can't hold up. They're getting sick from being treated like sardines. No problem. Bathe the meat in ammonia. So we now have genetically modified meat, bathed in ammonia and injected with antibiotics, neither of which would be needed if they were raised in the natural way.

If the corporations that run feedlots are the villains, Joel Salatin is the savior. Salatin's philosophy is to let animals thrive in a "symbiotic cycle of chemical-free feeding."[2] This means his cows feed on healthy grass and are moved from pasture to pasture rather than corn-fed in one central location. The chickens are brought in behind the cattle in portable coops, not kept in enormous, dark enclosures like the chicken houses run by the big companies. Salatin also refuses to sell to anyone outside of a four-hour drive of his farm in an effort to help people keep their money in their communities. "We think there is strength in decentralization and spreading out rather than in being concentrated and centralized," he said in an interview a few years ago.[3] For Joel Salatin, being a farmer is about being personal and local.

Joel Salatin may be a farmer, but for the people who are troubled by the modern food industry, he is a prophet, a voice crying in the wilderness. And in his view, he's being persecuted like a prophet too.

"Make no mistake," he told Michael Pollan, "we're in a war with the bureaucrats, who would like nothing better than to put us out of business."[4] Pollan spent time with Salatin in the process of researching and writing *The Omnivore's Dilemma*. Pollan wasn't sure if Salatin was being hyperbolic, but he didn't have much time to decide. Salatin's "full-blown prairie populist stemwinder" had begun.[5]

"The USDA is being used by the global corporate complex to impede the clean-food movement," Salatin continued.[6] The clean-food movement is the movement that Salatin and others are part of that values ecology over efficiency, complexity and interdependence over standardization and mechanization. It's small local farms raising crops and livestock in life-honoring, chemical- and hormone-free ways. But they're being shut down under what Salatin considers false pretenses, and Salatin is quite sure big-money corporate lobbyists have a hand in it. "They aim to close down all but the biggest meat processors, and to do it in the name of biosecurity. Every government study to date has shown that the reasons we're having an epidemic of food-borne illness in this country is centralized production, centralized processing, and long-distance transportation of food."[7]

Salatin is convinced that farms like his are especially vulnerable to temperamental government food officials because they pose a threat to a well-oiled, well-funded system that values efficiency and profit over everything else, even the health of its citizens. And he may be right.

What may surprise you is that Salatin is a devout Christian. His faith is not a disconnected spiritual life that he practices only in prayer and worship on Sundays. For Joel Salatin, it is his faith in the Creator-God that shapes his approach to farming. He tries to replicate the "model God used in building nature"[8] as he lets cows feed on grass while fertilizing it, and chickens serve as pest-control (they eat bugs) while they supplement the fertilization. The result is better beef, chicken, eggs, and crops—and healthier humans!—all because he's paying attention to the eco-rhythms the Creator built into His creation. Perhaps Salatin takes seriously the covenant God made with "every living creature" in Genesis 9.

Whatever the case, his faith has shaped his farming, and both have posed a threat to the system.

Start a Revolution?

There's a lot of talk these days about starting a revolution. Christians want to "revolutionize church" or start a "love revolution." It's exciting talk. It's the stuff that sounds good ringing through the speakers of a massive arena, especially when spoken by a dude with skinny jeans and messy hair, with strains of an electric guitar vamping over pulsing drums. And maybe in a cool accent. It's inspiring. Songs become anthems, sermons become sound bites, and phrases become rallying cries....

In the frenzy of youthful optimism, the most overlooked, under-asked question is, *Against whom are we revolting?* And furthermore, what does it look like to revolt against it? Then finally, what is the price of such a revolt?

It may not look like Joel Salatin rejecting corporate greed and the violation of ecology by running a small local farm, but it may mean thinking more carefully about where the food we eat comes from and at what expense to the worker and the earth. I recently finished doing premarital counseling for a young couple who chose not to use a diamond in the girl's engagement ring just to ensure that they wouldn't inadvertently support conflict diamonds. I know a young banker who refuses to depersonalize his clients by rushing them through the system just so he can meet a quota.

What do all these things have to do with faith in Christ?

The great Swiss theologian Karl Barth once wrote: "To clasp the hands in prayer is the beginning of an uprising against the disorder of the world."[9] Many Christians get the sense of this in the way they rally to oppose abortion or same-sex marriage or teenage immorality. And certainly, all that is part of the uprising against the disorder of the world. But there is more.

The "world" in the New Testament is used in two ways: It is either describing the universe—as in the cosmos, the totality of God's originally good creation; or it means the systems and structures and societies of people who have organized themselves apart from God and, indeed, against Him. This second sense of the "world" is often typified in prophetic language as "Babylon." Babylon, in bibli-cal parlance, is the epitome of a system, structure, and society that has raised itself up independently of and against God. Early in the

Genesis story, the tower of Babel itself is a picture of man's systematic, structural, and societal revolt. It is human rebellion beyond the individual level of Eden; it is a full-blown *coup d'état* against God and His rule. In the dramatic closing book of the Bible, John's vision paints a stunning picture of contrasting unequal parts: the reigning Lamb versus the eventually defeated Beast; the spotless Bride in contrast to the vile Whore; and Jerusalem, God's shining city, set against Babylon, the organized godlessness of the world. There is Jesus and His kingdom and His people. And there is the pathetic parody that is ultimately destroyed.

To take Barth's words seriously, we must understand that prayer is about recognizing Jesus as the true King of the world, and that belief in Jesus as King demands a certain way of living. If the people of God believe that the "earth is the LORD's and the fullness thereof" (Ps. 24:1 ESV), then we will care that the earth is being abused. If we believe that Jesus is the only Lord over all, then we will follow and obey Him here and now. If we believe that the Way of Jesus and His kingdom run in opposition to the values of the systems and structures of the world, then we must think more carefully about what systems and structures of evil and oppression we are complicit in.

But I cannot tell you what that *should* look like in its particulars. That is part of your embracing the King and His kingdom. Every area—*every* area: how we treat others, where we buy our food and clothing, the way we vote, and the way we work—must be brought under God's reign. And that may take on different hues on each individual canvas. We must not stand as anyone's judge. But each must raise the questions and wrestle through to answers. And then wrestle through again and again until Messiah returns.

True, there is much that we cannot undo or fully set right. But, as I will attempt to explain in the epilogue, we should get on with doing what we can rather than throw up our hands in resignation. To be clear, our goal is not to create utopia here. And yet we are to anticipate the kingdom coming in fullness by living now the way it will be then. I will say much more about that in the next chapter.

Enough clumsy foreshadowing. If we are not being rejected by the systems and structures of a world that has organized itself apart from and against God, perhaps it is because we have not yet rejected them. We pose no threat. Perhaps we have not yet embraced the kingdom of God; we have only gotten comfortable with a religion that has a shell of godliness but has denied its power.

Lucky are those who are rejected by the world, for they are a threat to it and their reward is from a kingdom not of this world.

DISCUSSION QUESTIONS

1. What does it mean to live in opposition to the world—i.e., the systems, structures, and societies that are independent of and against God?

2. What's the difference between living in opposition to the world and being obnoxious? Is it possible to live against the grain of culture while living "quiet, peaceable lives"?

3. In a culture of selfishness and depersonalization, where people are treated like "things" or "functions," how do we live in a different way? How do you live differently in your vocation?

4. Have you ever experienced the consequences of living in opposition to the world?

CHAPTER SEVEN

LUCK-BEARERS

He doesn't know her name or her story. He doesn't know that he will meet her or that, in less than a week, her words will leave him undone. Right now, after a long red-eye from Denver to JFK, everything is a bit fuzzy. *Is the queasiness from a lack of sleep, or is it the anxiety that I'm feeling?* It's hard to keep his thoughts straight. He's not altogether certain what he's getting himself into. It occurs to him that he is only a short drive from his parents' house in north Jersey. *Do I really want to get on this flight?* The seven-hour layover in JFK's worn-down international terminal is twisting the knot in his stomach.

But he can't shake the conviction that he *needs* to get on that plane; this trip is somehow meant to be part of his destiny. As the cabin doors close and the wheels of the Airbus A340 lift up from the tarmac, he glances out the window, watching the city he has seen so many times as a child begin to slowly light up with life. *Eighteen hours from New York to Johannesburg. Good God, I'm going to Africa.* It's not the quickest way to get to Entebbe, Uganda, but they booked their tickets late, and the cheapest route was also quite possibly the longest.

Closing his eyes, trying to settle into his seat—the one he is going to be in for the next eighteen hours—he feels his soul starting to collapse. The past few months have been exhausting. He just finished writing the songs and recording guitar and lead vocals for his band's fifth album, their first studio project and his first as coproducer. *Why was that such a lonely experience?*

The band began with three worship leaders and songwriters in 2002. But in the past year, two of them felt it was time to move on and that he was the one to lead it into the next phase of its identity. So in the spring of 2009, when the Desperation Band began preparing for a studio project, the weight of choosing the right songs, the right arrangements, and the right production approach lay heavy on Jon Egan's shoulders. Releasing a project without the other two worship leaders left him feeling exposed, open to criticism he would have to bear alone.

Riffs and grooves click on and off in his head beyond his control. Scenes of the rehearsals, the conversations, and the agonizing scrutiny of signing off on each final mix start playing in his mind more clearly than the in-flight movie. *So this is how the next eighteen hours are going to be?*

When he was handed the finished master just yesterday—*or was it the day before?*—he should have felt relieved. Instead he felt abused—by himself, by the journey, by the voices in his head. People came up to him asking how he felt about it and if he was excited. *I feel like I just finished a marathon without training for it and collapsed in a ditch on the side of the road.* He wasn't being cynical. He was being honest. Now that emotional emptiness feels more hollow than a burned-out star because of a lack of sleep and his entrapment in a flying steel tube.

And the child behind him kicking his seat isn't helping.

———

He turns to his right and sees the face of a faithful friend across the aisle, a friend whose eyes have spoken more encouragement over the years than a thousand tales could tell. Jeremiah Parks is of above-average height, though you can't tell that by the way he's slumped in his chair. He keeps refolding his sinewy frame to fit within the allotted space between rows. Looking at Jon, he smiles. And with that smile comes comfort, reassurance, and a reminder of why they are going to Uganda.

A little over a year ago, their high school ministry, _tag, began a journey that seemed impossible. Jon, Jeremiah, and Brent, the youth pastor, were looking for ways to get their students to look beyond themselves, to see a world outside their own struggles. Jeremiah had thought of the idea of raising money to build an orphanage. When Jeremiah called Kirby, a good friend and businessman and dad to one of _tag's students, to discuss the idea, Kirby simply said, "The Father has already spoken to me about this. They're not going to build one home; they're going to build four." Kirby has a major passion for orphan care, and the project struck a chord with him. After estimating the costs with the help of a ministry called World Orphans, they figured they needed about thirty thousand dollars to build one home. Kirby agreed to match whatever they raised, but still, how much could several hundred high school kids raise? In eight weeks _tag raised over sixty thousand dollars, and Kirby, true to his word, matched every dollar.

But the journey was so much more than a fund-raising campaign. It became about students rescuing students; it was about a young American generation, "orphaned" by divorce, abuse, or simply absence, reaching beyond themselves to a Ugandan generation that was literally orphaned by AIDS. It was about destiny rescuing destiny. They were calling it Heartwork.

Now a team of teenagers, a few college-age leaders, and a couple of staffers from _tag are already in Uganda to see the first orphan home they had raised funds to build, working with a Ugandan ministry called the Father's Divine Love Ministries (affectionately referred to as simply FDLM) in the remote town of Jinja, digging trenches, clearing fields, and helping to build a few homes for widows. Jon signed on to this trip to see it for himself and to help others see it by capturing it on film. Because of his platform with the Desperation Band, Jon became a voice for Heartwork. But in the last few months, things were moving quickly, and he didn't want to merely champion a cause. He wanted to participate in it. *That's why I'm doing this. That's why I'm on this plane.*

Jeremiah gets up from his seat and slides in on Jon's left, leaving Kirby to try bending his large frame over two seats in a hundred different ways with moderate success. Jon and Jeremiah talk in short, weighty sentences. *Crazy, isn't it? Look at where this whole thing is going!* A few laughs. Heads shake in amazement. Eyes close. The wheels bounce on something firm, then race toward a finish line. Lights brighten. An alarm dings softly. *OK, we're in Africa.*

Yet all three of them know they must wait another seven hours in this airport before catching a five-hour flight to Entebbe. But the excitement of being closer is mitigating their exhaustion.

As the smaller South African Airways plane approaches the long road Entebbe calls its runway, it's been almost two full days since Jon, Jeremiah, and Kirby left Denver International Airport. Peering out the window, Jon can't tell if he's dreaming. The scene looks lifted from *National Geographic*. On either side of the runway is red dirt, kicked up into mini-cyclones by dozens of dark-skinned children. Some are wearing shoes, some are riding rusted bicycles. None of them have clothes that fit. A few are in what look to be school uniforms, with fragments of what once were sandals on their feet. In the distance are women in colorful one-piece garments, with cloths that cover their heads like a bandanna, less as an accessory and more as a necessity in the heat. They have large water jugs braced on their shoulders. As Jon makes his way down the steps of the plane onto the worn-down tarmac, squinting into the setting sun, the children stare. They are curious. They are laughing. They are happy. The women glance over but have seen this scene too many times to read hope into the arrival of a stranger. The few feet that separate the red dirt from the shiny metal bird carrying visitors from richer lands seems a like chasm between two worlds.

And the barbed-wire fence isn't helping.

Everybody Cares

Why do we care about injustice?

It's slightly amusing that a culture that insists on no rules when it comes to morality, particularly sexual morality, is quite vocal about some other rules, like ending human trafficking or making trade fair. It is difficult to be a part-time moral relativist and a part-time social activist. You simply can't have it both ways. Either there is evil in the world—and consequently in our hearts!—or there isn't.

But most of the time, the conversations and campaigns to do good things don't probe beneath the surface. The underpinning philosophy is never questioned. The beginning assumption is that we *all* do care—indeed, that we all *should* care.

Even the NBA cares. So they tell us. With footage, set to heart-tugging music, of all-stars and benchwarmers teaching underprivileged children to dribble a basketball, I'm almost convinced. No doubt pro athletes do a lot to give back to their communities, and organizations like the United Way and the Boys and Girls Clubs have found a way to harness their soft hearts and deep pockets. Now scattered through every televised NBA game are specially crafted commercials with players from the teams you're watching—extending aid, rebuilding communities, and effectively persuading you that the NBA cares.

But when did caring become a campaign?

Social justice is all the rage. Starbucks sells water bottles that donate a portion of their proceeds to help provide clean water in areas of the world that are without it. American Apparel boasts "sweatshop-free" clothes. GAP, Apple, Microsoft, American Express, Converse, and a slew of other multinational corporate giants have joined the (RED) campaign, an initiative begun in part by U2 front man, Bono, in an effort to raise money for the fight against AIDS. The charge to bring justice to the helpless and aid to the poor is being championed by street-corner poets and opportunistic politicians, bohemian rock bands and bourgeois suburbanites. From collegiate halls to corporate boardrooms, the reality of exploitation is unveiled, and the challenge is being issued to bear the burden of solving the injustices and improving life for people around the world.

And all that is a good thing. A very good thing. To some extent, it doesn't matter whether a company is motivated by greed or altruism so long as they do something to help. But as more people and organizations join the movement to change the world one pair of Chuck Taylors at a time, the question of why we feel this sense of *ought* needs to be explored. Where does this impulse to help, to improve life for others, to right the injustices in the world come from?

In the NBA's case, it might have been from a desire to fix its public image. The 1980s were a Golden Age of sorts for the NBA, with Larry Bird and Magic Johnson carrying their collegiate rivalry to the ultimate stage, reviving images of the old Russell-Chamberlain, Lakers-Celtics rivalry of a bygone era. It was hard to imagine the game getting any bigger than that. And yet, in the 1990s, it did. Michael Jordan, long accused of being too selfish, too much of a scorer to ever win a ring, led his Chicago Bulls to six championships in eight years. And there might have been more if Jordan hadn't taken a brief break from the game to grieve his father's death. In the Jordan years, seemingly everybody watched basketball. There was the sense that we were watching the greatest basketball player of all time in his prime. As the lights on Jordan's legendary career faded, the new Laker duo of Shaq and Kobe—coached by Jordan's Zen-master himself, Phil Jackson—was making fans believe that the NBA was destined to go from glory to glory. While baseball struggled to be drug-free and football saw the end of dynasties, basketball was quickly becoming America's sport, with a global audience paying close attention.

Then, as a new century began, things began to fall apart. Shaq and Kobe split ways. Jackson resigned. Egos swelled and broke through the surface of the NBA's Hollywood skin like an untimely pimple. The league was not as innocent as we had thought. At the 2004 Summer Olympics in Sydney, Australia, a team of hot-shot American all-stars displayed only arrogance and immaturity as they self-destructed before the world, failing to take the gold for the first time since Magic, Bird, and Jordan formed the first American Dream Team in 1992.

Then, in Detroit on November 19, 2004, the bottom finally fell out. With less then a minute to go in a game between the Pacers and the Pistons, a skirmish broke out between players from both teams. It was little more than a shoving match accentuated by a few theatrical taunts until a fan threw a cup of Diet Coke at Ron Artest, who played for the Indiana Pacers at the time. Artest climbed up into the stands and threw a punch at the fan he—mistakenly—thought had assaulted him. Artest's teammate Stephen Jackson followed him, landing a few blows of his own on Piston fans. When the melee was finally over, the league and its players, coaches, and fans were in shock. An ESPN poll reported that 83 percent of their fans regarded it as "the ugliest incident of fan-player violence" they had ever seen.[1] Nine players were suspended, five of whom were charged with assault and sentenced to a year on probation with community service.

Almost a year later, in October 2005, the NBA introduced its own self-imposed sentence of community service. They called the campaign NBA Cares.

So when a corporation or a church does things to help the poor or reverse injustice, it's hard not to wonder if it isn't simply another public-relations campaign. For Christian organizations, is this concern for the poor a thinly veiled attempt to shed the old, angry Bible-thumping preacher image and replace it with a kinder, gentler Christianity? Less Old Time Gospel, more Mother Teresa?

Or maybe it's not public relations. Maybe it's cultural imperialism. This phrase has long been leveled against missionaries and Christian foreign-aid workers but could now well apply to many mainstream social justice efforts. After all, what gives someone—a corporation, a band, a Peace Corps worker—the right to say to another culture, another country, another corporation that what they are doing must stop? On what basis does an American company tell a man who runs a brothel in Bangkok that his business is *wrong?* What grounds does a college professor stand on when he wags his finger at the treatment of workers in Cambodia? What makes Chris Martin, the lead singer of Coldplay, the authority on trade laws?

What we want to say is that injustice is simply *just wrong.* That selling children for sex is a violation of human dignity, that forcing underpaid workers to operate under harsh conditions is dehumanizing and soul-destroying. And it is.

But *why* do we think that? On what basis can we say that? How do the same professors who claim moral relativity when they choose to sleep with a grad student pretend to have a sort of universal moral authority when it comes to trade and justice? If ethics and morality are simply a matter of preference, who's to say the powerful Western nations who control the media and the classroom aren't simply imposing their preferences on the rest of the world?

If you believe in no god, you would have to perform some impressive acrobatics of logic to provide ethical or moral grounds unrooted in some sort of divine being or force. If you believe in a vague Spirit or Force, then your beef with the injustices of the world is that it violates the "way of the universe." But if the Life Force of Spirit permeates all things, is It not as present in "the mud and the marble impartially"?[2] Is the Life Spirit not in men we call good and men we call evil? How then should we say that certain people— Hitler, Khomeini, Pol Pot, etc.—are bad and that their actions are wrong, while certain other people—Buddha, Jesus, Gandhi, etc.— are good and that their teachings should be followed? What makes a teacher, let alone his teachings, good?

And again, why do we care about injustice?

Uganda: Day 1

She has no idea what's coming.

For most of her life, her family considered her an outcast. With kids to raise and no husband to help, Ruth is among the many helpless widows in Uganda. But Ruth is different. She believes in a God who cares for her, a God who sees her need. And for that, her family despises her. The very idea of a God who rescues is ridiculous to her family. They tell her repeatedly that she is foolish, that no god will ever rescue her, that she is doomed to live like this forever.

Her mother, Rusty, shares Ruth's faith but can do little else to help. There are only two main seasons in Uganda: dry or wet. And the wet season can be torrential. Many times in those stormy months,

Ruth's feeble, makeshift hut would shake violently with the winds as rain came spilling down on their mud floors. The darkness would be struck by a radiant flash shining on the terrified faces of her young children. And just as their gleaming, fearful eyes faded to black, the thunder bellowed like an angry god. In those moments she would think, *What if my family is right? What if there is no god who sees me, no god who cares about my difficulty?*

Still, in those moments she prays for rescue. Always praying for rescue.

And deep down she believes that it's helping.

———

On their first morning in Uganda, Jon, Jeremiah, and Kirby head off to the remote town of Jinja. Getting there is like a scene from an *Indiana Jones* movie, sans the lasso and the safari outfits. From Entebbe, their minibus zooms past bicycles and trucks, families on mopeds, and dark green foliage and deep red earth for four hours until they arrive at the sugarcane fields of Jinja. They spent the night before in a hotel of sorts in Entebbe, their first night in a bed in three nights. So the morning has all the promise of a new day, fueled by the adrenaline of finally arriving at their long-awaited destination. To top it off, being surrounded by unbridled nature in the wildness of Africa is giving this whole thing the vigor of a Hemingway story.

As they get close to Jinja, sugarcane fills the horizon from east to west, which makes the gap in the fields even more noticeable. When the minibus approaches, the gap slowly fills in with tall figures that seem to slow down the closer they get. The sight of their team pushing wheelbarrows, slopping a muddy mixture onto the framed outline of a hut with a makeshift tool almost makes Jon, Jeremiah, and Kirby burst into tears. In a strange way, they feel at home.

Though they are freshly showered and the team is caked in dirt, they embrace each teammate like they've just won Olympic gold. Half the team is on the other side of Jinja, they learn, about a thirty-minute drive from here. They had split the team up to work on clearing the fields and digging trenches for a handful of different homes. The newcomers are assigned to the team on the other side of Jinja.

More zooming past bicycles and trucks and families on mopeds. More sugarcane fields with a clearing sparsely filled by American teenagers. More hugs and laughs and tears. Then someone throws Jon a pair of gloves and he starts to dig. *How could manual labor feel so good?* There under the African sun, the pressure from the previous months falls from him like the sweat from his brow. Months of agonizing over the album, of trying to prepare himself for the unrelenting opinions of reviewers and critics, all start to feel like years ago. The fears and doubts crumble and are tossed aside like the dirt from his shovel. Women in colorful garments walk by with jugs of water on their shoulders. He waves. They wave back. The world seems to be in harmony.

That night they are taken to the Father's Divine Love Ministries (FDLM). The first things they see as they approach the compound are tall concrete walls with iron gates. But the pastor of FDLM, a muscular Ugandan man appropriately named David Livingstone, explains that the walls and gates aren't there to keep the kids in; they're there to keep kidnappers and vandals out. In Jinja it is well known that FDLM gets funding from American churches and ministries and has a few nice things as a result. What's more terrifying is the fact that a renegade terrorist group, blasphemously named the Lord's Redemption Army, views kidnapping orphans as a means of recruiting soldiers. This compound has homes for the orphans, a cafeteria building of sorts, and a church.

When the gates swing open and their minibus pulls into the courtyard, kids in mismatched clothes begin to gather. They crowd around the *mzungus*, the white-skinned visitors. "Watz yur nem?" a child says softly to Jon. He answers and asks her the same question. She replies and looks away with a giggle. Others come and repeat the ritual. Some stand aside and watch, not from disinterest but from shyness. Several, without speaking, tug at his clothes as a silent way of saying, "We're glad you're here." Jon responds with a wordless gesture of his own: His tears are now streaming down his face.

And the hope in their eyes and the joy in their hearts are helping.

New Creation Now

Why do we care about injustice? What gives us the grounds to say to someone else that what they are doing is wrong and that it must stop? What makes people praise the teachings of Jesus, Buddha, and Gandhi but condemn the words of Hitler, Stalin, and Khomeini? The Christian has a way of responding to these questions. It is not by saying that *everyone* prefers justice because God wired him or her to do so, though that may be true. It is rooted in a story much wider than that simple statement. In this story we find a wellspring for mercy and justice far deeper than corporate guilt or public relations or cultural imperialism. This story tells us things about God and humanity and creation that we may have suspected but never fully realized.

God created the heavens and the earth. He called it good. He made every living thing in both heaven and earth. And then He made Human.

This much we know. But before you jump ahead to the bit about sin, ask yourself a question: Why did He make Human? Again you'll have to momentarily silence the familiar chorus that "God made mankind to be in relationship with Him." True. But Genesis doesn't say that. What it does say is that God made humanity, first, to be in His image, and second, to reign. N. T. Wright explains it best:

> [Creation] was designed as a project, created in order to go somewhere. The creator has a future in mind for it; and Human … is the means by which the creator is going to take his project forward.… The point of the project is that the garden be extended, colonizing the rest of creation; and Human is the creature put in charge of that plan.… God placed Human in the garden to reflect His image into the new world he was making—that is, to be the means, present and visible, whereby his own care of the garden and the animals would become a reality.[3]

The goal of the first humans was that, in fellowship and communion with God, they would be God's image-bearers and bring His wise order and loving rule to the world.

Now we can get to the part we know. Adam and Eve sinned. They rebelled, and as a result of that rebellion, evil infected the cosmos. We have said all this and more in chapter 2. We have also discussed at length in the earlier chapters about Christ's role: how He came and shared in our sufferings, took the worst blow evil could give, and by rising again, defeated it, draining the poison from evil's sting and atoning for humanity's sin all in one triumphant stroke.

It is worthwhile to take a small diversion from our big story to mention the reason we as Christians give more weight to Christ's words than to Gandhi's. Christians trust the teachings of Christ because we receive them as being from God, for Jesus is God incarnate. His teachings are *good* because they are rooted in His person, and His person is *good* for He is God. The Christian would say, then, that inasmuch as the teachings of Gandhi or Buddha approximate the teachings of Christ, they are good. But they are not good on their own grounds or in themselves. And even if they are good and true and right in the ways they approximate what Christ said, they still do not carry the ability to transform, nor does the demand for the hearer to conform to their words come from God incarnate. It is the belief in the incarnation that frames our view of Christ's teachings as truth. They are not from God because they are true; they are true because they are from God. None of the other good, moral teachers made this claim, leaving a spiritualist or an atheist without a firm basis for calling their teachings *good*, even though many of the pieces are.

Back to the story. Jesus, the God-Man, perfectly fulfilled the call of the first human: He is the "image of the invisible God" and the world's true King. Now because of Him, the redeemed humanity—those who are in Him—recover the original vocation given to humans: to be priests and rulers. We share in the reign of Jesus, a reign that will result ultimately in the renewal of the whole world. Remember in chapter 5, when we talked about new creation, the day when Yahweh makes a new heaven and a new earth? It is the clear hope we have for the future as glimpsed by John's Revelation. The end of the story is like the beginning: God's redeemed "new humanity" will reign with Him over His new heaven and new earth, joined together at last.[4]

It is not simply about getting my soul saved. It is about getting humans back in right standing before God so that His work of new creation can begin in them and so that they then can bring His wise order and loving rule to the new world in the age to come. Any picture of salvation that is less than new creation in this sweeping sense is a bit anemic. To tell this big story as a set of spiritual laws is like explaining a Tchaikovsky symphony as a mathematical sequence of intervals: It may be true, but you're losing the grandeur. To make the gospel only about personal salvation is like trying to replicate a Rembrandt on an Etch A Sketch: You may get the picture, but you're missing the beauty.

Unless you grasp this broad framework of God's first creation and the first humans' role in it along with God's new creation and the redeemed humanity's role in it, you won't know how to make sense of working to right injustice. You'll think it's all sort of good works that a Christian ought to do because Jesus said something or other about it. Or, worse, you'll dismiss it as a mere social agenda like the man at our church who said, "Please! Let's not talk about human trafficking and helping the poor. Let's get on with getting souls saved." When all we've

focused on is Jesus "dying for our sins so we can go to heaven," it is difficult to know why we ought to care about injustice. *Aren't we all going
to fly away anyway?* But if you have a clear picture of how the story
began and a compelling vision of its conclusion, the middle—our time
on earth now—makes more sense.

If we believe that when "God redeems the whole creation,
redeemed humans will play the key role, resuming the wise, healing
sovereignty over the whole world for which God made them in the
first place,"[5] then your view of the here and now begins to change.

When a Christian talks about helping the poor and extending
mercy to the helpless, he is not engaging in a public-relations campaign, but he *is* reclaiming an Image; she is not imposing her cultural
values on another region of the world, but she *is* recovering the call
to carry blessing to all peoples. For the Christian, justice and mercy
are not fashionable ideas that can fuel a clever campaign and give
our church folks a sense of purpose and a nice feeling of fulfillment.
Carrying hope to the hopeless, being a blessing to all peoples is our
original design, a design now restored to us in Christ.

Why do we care about injustice? Because God's new creation has
begun in us. The work that God will do to remake earth and heaven has
begun now in the renovation of our hearts by the Holy Spirit. Every time
that renewing work spills out into beginning to set things right in our
world, we are anticipating the kingdom that is coming. We are letting
God's will through us be "done on earth as it is in heaven" (Matt. 6:10).

In sports, players are taught to anticipate an opponent's move.
A good defensive back in football will study game film to anticipate where the opposing quarterback will throw the ball. He studies
for hours and hours so that, on game day, he can *anticipate* it and

"jump the route." In basketball, when two teammates work on their chemistry, the one knows where to be at a particular moment; he is *anticipating* the pass. To anticipate is to go in advance: It is to go where the football is going before the quarterback releases it; it is to move without the basketball toward the basket because you know that's where the pass will be. Anticipating, for the Christian, is all about doing in advance what you know will be done. It is learning to "live in the present in the light of God's inbreaking future."[6]

Disciples of Jesus were called Christians in Acts as a way of saying that they were "little Christs." But "Christ," especially in first-century Jewish circles, was a way of saying "Messiah." Were Jesus' followers, then, being called "mini-Messiahs"? We are called "the body of Christ" (1 Cor. 12:27). But the phrase is so familiar, it may have lost some of its zing. Would it be closer to Paul's intent to say that we are "Messiah's body," the people through whom Messiah, by His Spirit, is at work on the earth? And if all that, then we must ask this: If Messiah will set the world right, free the oppressed, end war—and do all the other things that Isaiah saw—when He returns, how should we live in the meantime?

Every time we give a cup of cold water in Jesus' name, every time we help the poor, every time we release people from oppression, we are announcing and anticipating the kingdom of God. We are living as *luck-bearers*.

Uganda: Day 5

It's now their fifth day in Uganda, their fourth in Jinja. Today, they are told, is going to be special. In the morning, Jon, Jeremiah, and the entire team go to dedicate the very first orphan home that _tag had raised funds to build. They haven't showered since arriving, and the baby wipes can only get so much red dirt off their quickly bronzing skin. When they arrive at the home, they are struck by the care and detail with which it was made. It is the nicest building they have seen yet by far. The kids moved in a few weeks ago, and their eyes are beaming with gratitude. Pastors from all across Jinja have gathered to thank God for this new home. A translator helps the Americans understand what is being said and prayed. Jeremiah gets up to share, and the same translator turns English into Luganda.

After lunch with the children, Jon and Jeremiah leave to talk to a handful of believers who live in the bush. The drive is on difficult terrain, and the scene when they arrive resembles a *Survivor* tribal council in an unsettling way. Nevertheless, standing around a fire, Jeremiah shares from the Scriptures, his ragged beard now glistening with the dancing sparks. When "church" is over, Jon and Jeremiah return to the FDLM compound and quickly run over to meet the rest of the team.

They are at a small, newly completed home about three hundred yards away. As their lungs work overtime trying to extract oxygen from the thick night air, they slowly peer inside. It would be a hut by American standards. But the walls are stronger than the shanties they've seen here in Jinja. And the roof is sturdy and sealed, and the floor is not just earth and mud. This is, by all counts, a bona fide house. A small, square, African house.

It's dark in the house. The only light is from a video camera one of the team members brought with him. The team has filled in along the sides, allowing only a small space in the center as a stage of sorts. There is a woman in the middle. She looks to be in her mid-thirties, but her face shows the wear of more sorrow than a woman twice her age. Her hair is pulled back under a brightly colored bandanna, like so many Ugandan women. And like so many Ugandan women, she's wearing a one-piece garment that swirls with color.

Her name is Ruth. Next to Ruth is a woman who is gesturing encouragement toward Ruth like a mother over a child. She is Ruth's mother. Ruth's children are on the other side. They look young. Their eyes are wide.

David Livingstone, the young Ugandan pastor, is also standing with them. He faces them, then the team, then them again, talking, telling Ruth's story. He tells of her struggle, of her faithfulness. He announces that this house is now hers. He prays over her, dedicating the home to the Lord.

Jon is in a corner of the home, watching, trembling. He is by a window that is barred from the inside. Outside, small, dark faces of children peer in with white curious eyes and teeth that gleam in the darkness.

Then Ruth begins to speak. She was an outcast to her family. She was ridiculed for having nothing. People counted her a fool for believing that God would come to her rescue. Many nights, when the rain relentlessly abused her feeble hut of stick and straw, she would cry out, "I have been told that You are the Father to the fatherless and Husband to the widow.… So, rescue us!"

How many times has Jon heard or sung or read that God was a Father to the fatherless, a Husband to the widow? Yet from the lips of a widow in Africa who had no means of saving herself, it was as if these words are new. The days leading up to this one have had hints of Ruth's name. He knew that, at some point, they would be giving a home to this woman. But nothing could have prepared him for this moment. Her voice keeps ringing in his head: *I have been told that You are the Father to the fatherless and Husband to the widow....*

Ruth is emotional but not tearful. Her eyes are sunken from exhaustion. Something about her seems familiar to Jon. She looks bone-weary, like she has just finished a marathon without training for it and is lying in a ditch on the side of the road.

Her voice breaks his thoughts, her actual voice: "And now I stand here with a secure roof over my head, a floor beneath my feet, secure walls ... and I thank God because He heard my cry and He rescued me!"

A large shadow moves to the center of the room. His head is bent down and his walk is slow. It is Kirby. With the help of a translator, he says, in sure, deliberate words, "The Father has spoken to me ... and I promise you that you ... will never have another need ... for the rest of your life...."

He is shaking. "We will personally see that your kids will be taken care of ... and will be put in school...."

He reaches in his pocket, pulls out a faded green note of American currency, and says with dramatic finality, "Here ... is my down payment."

As he turns to walk back, sniffs and snobs crescendo in true surround sound. Jon is now breathing with short, deep breaths as his gut pulses with emotion. His body can no longer support the emotion his soul is carrying. Bones and joints collapse in a corner as if to mirror the pool running out of his eyes all over his face. If he could have looked up, he would have seen that everyone else was sobbing too.

Ruth is on her knees, shouting now in her native tongue. Her hands are raised and the meaning of her words is unmistakable: praise, gratitude, love for the Father, her Husband, the One who heard her cry and rescued her. Now Ruth is the worship leader. The whole room is erupting in un-melodic praise.

Jon is still unable to make his mouth form words. But he is able to listen. And it is God who starts to speak. *This is your healing.* In this moment—one of the most spiritually significant moments of his life—he knows that *this* was what it was all for. The band, the music, the influence has all been for Ruth, for these children, for the luckless. He is to carry luck to the unlucky, and none of the insecurities or fears or desires to control people's opinions of him can stand a chance against that. He is a luck-bearer.

When he finally stands up to walk out, Jeremiah, his own face muddy from dirt-mingled tears, catches him at the door. "Hey … while all that was happening … I just had the sense that … that *this* would be your healing."

Jon smiles at his friend and shakes his head in amazement. The healing has already begun, and it has begun in the most unlikely of places. Healing came as he carried the kingdom to the unlikely and the unlucky.

And the tears that she cried and the praise that was rising to heaven are helping.

DISCUSSION QUESTIONS

1. How many "justice" causes or campaigns are you aware of? How has the rise in popularity of such causes made you feel—numb, cynical, excited?

2. What is the Christian framework for working to end injustice?

3. In what ways can you "live in anticipation" of the kingdom's culmination? What actions can you take *this week?*

4. Have you ever experienced healing as you carried hope to someone else?

GOOD. LUCK.

We are lucky, for the kingdom of God—God's saving and sovereign rule through His covenant people—has come to us. We have gotten in on this great plan. We—simple, ordinary, common, weak, unlikely, and unlucky outsiders—are now the people of God! A comfort that is eternal and irreversible is ours. A fullness that satisfies all longing and makes every hunger disappear is coming. A reward from a kingdom that is not of this world is our long-awaited inheritance.

Moreover we have been invited to participate in God's single, sovereign, saving plan. We are called to announce and to anticipate the kingdom that is coming, which is a fancy way of saying we must now be luck-bearers to the unlucky.

But.

How?

There are so many who are unlucky. So much that is wrong with the world. Can we possibly set it right? Can we really reverse the fortunes of thousands—millions even!—of people?

Under New Management

Jesus told a puzzling story once. Well, several of His stories were puzzling, but this one is enigmatic even now.

The story is about a manager, a steward, which in the Roman world was a person who had access to his master's wealth and was an agent of his business affairs. The manager, though, had made a mess of things. He had "wasted his goods" (Luke 16:1 KJV). He was called by the master to give an account of his management and was informed that the position of management would be taken away from him. When the manager heard this, he decided on a plan. He went to all the people who owed his master money, debts he no doubt should have collected long ago, and offered them a discounted bill—not altogether unlike our modern creditors who will gladly take what they can get from a person in debt. "You owe a thousand dollars? Give me eight hundred, and we'll call it good." And on he went, trying to make things right. He couldn't fully undo the damage he had done; he could not collect the full amount of what was owed. But he did what he could, and Jesus praises him for his shrewdness.

Such praise seems strange. Wasn't the man being dishonest? Didn't Jesus imply that the manager was simply trying to ingratiate himself with the people who owed his master money in the event that he might need their assistance in the future? Isn't this like a guy who knows he's about to get fired from Apple giving away company secrets to Microsoft in the hopes of landing a job with them after his firing?

Not quite. For whatever other layers of lessons are in this parable, there is one that stands out clearly to me now; I have never quite noticed it before. The clue is in Jesus' closing remarks:

"Whoever can be trusted with very little can also be trusted with much, and whoever is dishonest with very little will also be dishonest with much. So if you have not been trustworthy in handling worldly wealth, who will trust you with true riches? And if you have not been trustworthy with someone else's property, who will give you property of your own?" (Luke 16:10–12)

Jesus, as recorded in Luke's gospel, has said something like this before. It appears in Luke 12: "From everyone who has been given much, much will be demanded; and from the one who has been entrusted with much, much more will be asked" (v. 48). There's that phrase again: *trusted with much*. In Luke 12, the story is about a master who will return at an unexpected hour. A wise and faithful manager is one who is taking care of the servants, getting them their food allowance and such in a timely fashion. That manager will be placed in charge of all the master's possessions. But the manager who gets impatient with the master's absence and decides to beat the servants and feast and get drunk will be severely punished.

In both stories, there is a master and a manager. And in both stories the manager will be held accountable for the things that were trusted to his care. If he manages them well, he will get to manage more—the antecedent, perhaps, of our modern maxim, "If you want something done, give it to the busy guy!" Both stories, when taken together, give us a picture of our human calling as stewards of God's world.

Humanity, beginning specifically with the first humans, was given charge of God's good world. But they squandered His treasure, and we have followed their example. Humans, meant to be God's agents, the viceroys of His estate, have instead made a mess of things. In our attempt to live like the sovereign, we have gotten drunk on the power and lost all resemblance to His rule. We have beaten the servants and wasted His possessions. We are the worst of both stories' depictions of a bad manager.

And yet. There is still time. Will we be shrewd enough, wise enough, to do what we can do, to try to set things right, even if not all the way? Clearly that is how we are to live as we wait for the Master's return. Jesus, in the earlier, less-enigmatic parable, said that the one "who knows his master's will and does not get ready or does not do what his master wants" would be punished severely (Luke 12:47). In that light it makes sense then that the apparently unjust manager who did what he could to set things right is praised by the master. *All right, so you've made a mess of things. And no, you can't truly set it right. But will you even try? Will you do what you can?*

Taken together, these stories of stewardship show us how to *anticipate* Christ's return. He is the Master; we are the managers. Everything in the world—the whole cosmos!—had been entrusted to mankind. By our original sin, we made a mess of things. And in doing so, we lost our place as managers. Chaos reigns; evil abounds. Even if we wanted to set things right, it is not within our power to fully do so. But there is One, fully God and fully human, who can. That is explained by another story the gospel writers told, a true one, of the Son of Man who went to the cross and gave His life "as a ransom for many" (Matt. 20:28). Because of Jesus, all who are in Him have recovered their original vocation as God's stewards. We have been re-entrusted with things. And since we know that the Master is returning, and we know how He runs His affairs, how should we as His servants manage His household in the in-between? Even as we wait for the Master's return, there are things that we can set right, even if it is not all the way. The only question that remains is this: Will the "people of the light" take a lesson from this shrewd manager of the world and do what they can to set things right in the meantime?

Will the world notice that redeemed humanity, the people of God, is living even now on the earth? Can anyone tell that the earth is, so to speak, under new management?

Butterfly Wings

A few years ago, I wrote a book called *Butterfly in Brazil*. The title is borrowed from the whimsical question a meteorologist in the 1970s raised as he was trying to explain chaos theory as it relates to weather systems: "When a butterfly flaps its wings in Brazil, does it create a tornado in Texas?"

I don't know much about weather systems or chaos theory. But I know that God has a habit of taking His people's small acts of obedience and faithfulness, lived out over the long haul, and using them to somehow propel His kingdom. I believed it when I wrote *Butterfly*, and I believe it even more strongly now.

What can God do with people who recognize the blessing that has come to them and understand the calling to carry it to the world?

What if we understood that we have not been made lucky for the sake of ourselves but for the sake of the unlucky?

What if we believed that the kingdom of God has come *to* us so that it can come *through* us?

What could happen if the people of God began to embrace the kingdom of God—if we announced its arrival and anticipated its culmination?

What if we began to live here on earth as it is in heaven, to live now as it will be then?

What if the lucky became luck-bearers?

After all we are *in* Jesus the Messiah; we are Messiah's body here on earth.

And because of that, we are not only *lucky.* We are, in Buechner's phrase, *the world's best luck.*

My favorite part of Psalm 10 in *The Message* reads:

> *Time to get up, GOD—get moving.*
> *The luckless think they're Godforsaken.*
> *They wonder why the wicked scorn God*
>   *and get away with it,*
> *Why the wicked are so cocksure*
>   *they'll never come up for audit.*

> *But you know all about it—*
>   *the contempt, the abuse.*
> *I dare to believe that the luckless*
>   *will get lucky someday in you.*
> *You won't let them down:*
>   *orphans won't be orphans forever.*

> *Break the wicked right arms,*
>   *break all the evil left arms.*

Search and destroy
  every sign of crime.
God's grace and order wins;
  godlessness loses.

The victim's faint pulse picks up;
  the hearts of the hopeless pump red blood
  as you put your ear to their lips.
Orphans get parents,
  the homeless get homes.
The reign of terror is over,
  the rule of the gang lords is ended. (vv. 12–18)

The reign of terror is over. The True King has come. His kingdom has touched down on earth. It has come to us, the unlikely and the unlucky, so that it might come through us to others who are unlikely and unlucky.

May it come through me. May it come through you. May it come through all of us together as the people of God on the earth even as we await the return of Jesus the Messiah.

NOTES

Chapter 1: Feeling Lucky?

1. Patricia Sullivan, "William 'Bud' Post III; Unhappy Lottery Winner," *The Washington Post*, January 20, 2006, www.washingtonpost.com/wp-dyn/content/article/2006/01/19/AR2006011903124.html.

2. Jesus spoke most often in Aramaic, which is quite similar to ancient Hebrew, and the closest Hebrew word to the Greek *makarios*, is *asar*. When the Old Testament, written originally in Hebrew, was translated into Greek a little before Jesus' time, they used *makarios* most often for the word *asar*. So it's fair to guess that Jesus used an Aramaic word that was a descendant, a derivative, of the Hebrew word *asar*.

3. Colin Brown, ed., *New International Dictionary of New Testament Theology, Vol. 1* (Grand Rapids, MI: Zondervan, 1986), 215.

4. The word for God blessing is *baruch*, as in Genesis 1:22: "God *blessed* them and said, 'Be fruitful and increase.'" The Greek equivalent for the Hebrew *baruch* to denote the God-blessed person would be *eulogia*.

5. Philip Yancey, *The Jesus I Never Knew* (Grand Rapids, MI: Zondervan, 1995), 107.

6. Luke 6:20b–22, slightly adapted NIV!

7. Jesus ascends a hill in Matthew's account; in Luke, the sermon takes place on a plain.

8. John R. W. Stott, *The Message of the Sermon on the Mount* (Leicester, England and Downers Grove, IL: InterVarsity, 1978), 37.

9. Dietrich Bonhoeffer, *The Cost of Discipleship* (New York: Macmillan Publishing Co., 1963), 118.

Chapter 2: Luck's Beginner

1. Charles Dickens, *Great Expectations* (New York: Barnes & Noble Classics, 2004), 133.

2. Rachel was the woman he wanted to marry; he was tricked into marrying Leah first, instead. Rachel had trouble conceiving so she gave her handmaiden to Jacob, as was customary. Leah did the same thing with her handmaiden. So, four women: two of them his wives, two of them their handmaidens. All of them lived within a culture not yet changed by God. While they obeyed His call, the process of learning this God and becoming like Him was slow.

3. Buechner has Isaac refer to God as "the Fear" perhaps because Isaac might have been introduced to this God as the one who asked his dad to sacrifice him. So Jacob would have learned that name from his father and followed suit in referring to God as the Fear. Buechner calls God the Shield of Abraham, the Fear of Isaac, and the Light of Jacob.

4. Frederick Buechner, *Son of Laughter* (New York: HarperCollins, 1994), 127.

5. Ibid., 251.

6. C. S. Lewis, *Miracles* (New York: Simon & Schuster, 1996), 156.

7. George Eldon Ladd, *The Gospel of the Kingdom* (Grand Rapids, MI: Eerdmans, 1959), 19.

8. Ibid.

9. N. T. Wright, *After You Believe* (New York: HarperCollins, 2010), 110.

10. Ibid., 114.

Chapter 3: The God-Dependent

1. Martin Luther, *Luther's Works, Vol. 21,* ed. Jaroslav Pelikan (St. Louis, MO: Concordia, 1956), 12.

2. Brown, ed., *New International Dictionary of New Testament Theology,* 215.

3. Luther, *Luther's Works,* 12.

4. R. T. France, *New International Commentary on the New Testament, The Gospel of Matthew* (Grand Rapids, MI: Eerdmans, 2007).

Chapter 4: Those Who Are Empty on the World

1. The full story I'm referencing is found in Luke 14:1–24.

2. C. S. Lewis, *Mere Christianity* (New York: HarperCollins, 2001), 136–137.

Chapter 5: Those Whose Best Life Isn't Now

1. It's impossible to talk like this and not acknowledge N. T. Wright, who has written extensively on the metaphor of exile and homecoming and how Israel's journey through that motif is a part of the larger picture of the whole cosmos in exile. (See *Simply Christian* and others of his works.)

2. Aleksandr Solzhenitsyn, *The Gulag Archipelago*, trans. Thomas P. Whitney (New York: Harper & Row, 1985), 312.

3. N. T. Wright, *Surprised By Hope* (London, England: SPCK, 2007), 93.

Chapter 6: Those Whom the World Rejects

1. "Welcome to Polyface, Inc.," Joel Salatin and Polyface, Inc., accessed October 12, 2010, www.polyfacefarms.com.

2. Ibid.

3. David E. Gumpert, "A New Push to Make Farming Profitable," *Bloomberg Businessweek*, August 10, 2007.

4. Michael Pollan, *The Omnivore's Dilemma* (New York: Penguin Press, 2006), 230.

5. Ibid.

6. Ibid.

7. Ibid.

8. Ibid., 215.

9. Karl Barth, *The Christian Life: Church Dogmatics*, IV.4 (Peabody, MA: Hendrickson).

Chapter 7: Luck-Bearers

1. Aleck Ryner and Brian Friel, "Uh-Oh's of the 00's: The Marvelous Mishaps of Sports," February 5, 2010, www.mhsmirador.com/sports/2010/02/05/uh-oh's-of-the-00's-the-marvelous-mishaps-of-sports/, accessed October 27, 2010.

2. Lewis, *Miracles*, 135.

3. Wright, *After You Believe*, 74–75.

4. For a text-by-text explanation of this in readable language, see Wright's *After You Believe*.

5. Wright, *After You Believe*, 91.

6. Ibid., 110.

Also from David C Cook and Glenn Packiam

Secondhand Jesus

Trading rumors of God for a firsthand faith.

1. Thursday

Life couldn't have been any better. We had been in our new house for just over a year, and it was almost time to start decorating for the holidays. Winter's frost was just blowing in over the Rocky Mountains. These were days of sipping hot chocolate and looking back over a year of steady church growth, rapidly expanding influence, and a company of close friends to enjoy it with. On top of all that, my wife, Holly, and I were expecting our second child, another girl. Life was good and there was no end in sight.

And then it was Thursday.

Everyone was distracted at work. There were meetings going on, first upstairs and then off campus, and later on campus in an impromptu staff meeting. Internet clips kept us glued to the screen as we tried desperately to decipher truth, accuracy, and some reason to believe the best. But as Thursday soldiered on, doubt was sitting lower and more heavily inside me.

I remember the feeling when I got home. My heart was kicking against my chest with frantic irregularity as I ran up the stairs to our room. The tightening knot in my stomach seemed to sink with each step. I opened our bedroom door, and with breathless shock sputtered, "Babe, some of it's true."

I had just returned from an elders' meeting where I learned that the seemingly absurd accusations leveled against our beloved pastor had enough truth in them to warrant his removal from office. On Friday, we learned that he would never be allowed back. By Sunday, we were sitting in church with hot tears racing down our faces, listening to letters that told us words we never thought we would hear. Our pastor had been a prominent national figure because of his role as president of the National Association of Evangelicals. He had been featured on Barbara Walters' program and other major news shows, had been called the most influential pastor in America. It was the biggest religious debacle in my lifetime. And it happened at my church. My church.

Thursday came and everything changed; my unshakeable "good life" became a nightmare of uncertainty. Would the church implode? Would everyone leave? Would I have a job next week? Could I ever get hired in ministry again? The songs, the influence, the success, the notoriety—it all became foolishly irrelevant.

Slowly, I replayed the past. The preceding years had been heady times. Our pastor's meteoric rise to the evangelical papacy paralleled the growing muscle of a conservative Christian movement now beginning to flex in the public square. The young men who had helped build our church, myself included, now found themselves swimming in much bigger circles of influence. We were talking to the press, traveling to Washington DC, and dropping more names than Old Testament genealogy. We had become powerful by association. And it was intoxicating. We were like the eager young men in Tobias Wolff's fictitious memoir of an elite prep school on the eastern seaboard, full of idealism and world-changing dreams.

It was a good dream and we tried to live it out, even while knowing that we were actors in a play, and that outside the theater was a world we would have to reckon with when the curtain closed and the doors were flung open.[1]

On Thursday, the theater doors flung open. The dream was over now. There was no thought of making an impact or changing the world. It was now about survival. How could we help our church stay intact?

As the days became weeks, it became clear that our church was made up of strong families who truly were connected to each other. It is a community akin to a small Midwestern town. So what if the mayor is gone? We're all still here. I watched men and women rally together in a heroic display of Christlike love.

It wasn't long before the shock of scandal gave way to the discomfort of introspection. This was ultimately not about a fallen pastor;

it was about fallen nature, a nature we all have lurking within us. It became less about the worst being true about him, and more about the worst being true about us. We began to allow the Lord to turn His spotlight, one more piercing than the light of any cameras, on our own hearts. Secret sins, recurring temptations, and hidden pride all looked sinister in His light. There was no such thing as a little white anything. Every weakness was now a dangerous monster with the potential of ruining our lives. Couples began to have difficult conversations with each other, friends became more vulnerable than they had ever been. Honest was the new normal. That sounds so strange to say.

But far beyond discussions and confessions, one question, one I never thought I would have trouble answering, relentlessly worked its way to my core. It surfaced from the pages of Henri Nouwen's book *In the Name of Jesus*. Nouwen had been an influential theology professor at Harvard, living at what most would have considered the apex of his career. But something was wrong.

> *After twenty years in the academic world as a teacher of pastoral psychology, pastoral theology, and Christian spirituality, I began to experience a deep inner threat. As I entered into my fifties ... I came face to face with the simple question, "Did becoming older bring me closer to Jesus?" After twenty-five years of priest-hood, I found myself praying poorly, living somewhat isolated from other people, and very much preoccupied with burning issues.*[2]

But Nouwen's inner wrestling was largely unnoticed by those around him, which made it more difficult for him to accurately gauge the condition of his heart.

Everyone was saying that I was doing really well, but some-
thing inside was telling me that my success was putting my own
soul in danger. I began to ask myself whether my lack of con-
templative prayer, my loneliness, and my constantly changing
involvement in what seemed most urgent were signs that the
Spirit was gradually being suppressed ... I was living in a very
dark place and ... the term "burnout" was a convenient psycho-
logical translation for spiritual death.[3]

Haunted by the emptiness of his own spiritual walk, Nouwen
started on a journey that eventually led to his resignation from
Harvard. He took a position as a chaplain at L'Arche, a care facility
for the handicapped. There he learned what it meant to live out a life
of love and servanthood, to live as Christ among the broken, to truly
"lead in the name of Jesus." I had read his profound and honest reflec-
tions years before, but as I reread them in the wake of the scandal,
I found myself convicted. Nouwen's question dealt with something
deeper than sin; it was about the essence of the Christian life, the thing
we must have above all else.

I remember sitting with a few friends in my living room on New
Year's Eve, reflecting on how insane 2006 had been. We decided to
have a little dessert and ponder the year that was now in its closing
hours. Each couple took turns reviewing highs and lows of the year.
For the most part, it had been a good year. Bigger and better opportunities, unexpected financial success, the births of healthy children,
and the accelerated elimination of debt were some of the items on
the good list. But we had also experienced Thursday, and "bigger
and better" now seemed as days long ago, *auld lang syne*. The events

of that day in November now overshadowed everything the next year might hold. Everything was good now, but how long would it continue? Would the things that had gone awry last year create repercussions that would undermine all the things we had held so dearly? For some, the fear of losing the jobs they loved was becoming a distinct possibility. The reality of how suddenly a curve in the road can appear was sobering us.

And then I raised The Question: Did we—did I—know Christ more as a result of the passing of another year? Were we any closer to God? It was not the sort of question to answer out loud. I wrestled with it in silence. It was a question of my own relationship with Christ.

I have been a Christian since I was a young boy. I spent my high school years sitting in on the Old Testament history classes my mom taught at our church's Bible college, listening to sermon tapes, and praying and planning with my dad as he and my mom planted a church. My youth was defined by long quiet times, meaningful journal entries, and leadership roles in our youth group. I was a theology major in college and had been in full-time, vocational ministry for six years. Yet in the wake of Thursday, none of this mattered. Did I truly know God … *today?* Was my knowledge of Him active and alive, or stale and sentimental?

There was no easy or succinct way to answer that question. But as I allowed it to burrow its way in my heart, I began to see something. I had long lived subconsciously believing that God was a sort of cosmic agent, working to get me bigger contracts and better deals while saving me from scammers and opportunists. God was my Jerry Maguire, my ambassador of quan, and my prayers were spiritually cloaked versions of asking Him to "show me the money." Not necessarily literal money—just comfort, success, good friends, an enjoyably smooth road, an unmitigated path to the peak of my game.

If you had suggested that theology to me, I would have condemned it, criticized it, and denied three times that I even knew of it. It wasn't until Thursday came and went that I saw what was lurking inside. I had slowly bought the suburban rumors of God. My house was an evidence of His blessing. Our growing church was an indication of God's pleasure. Things were going to get better and better while I kept my life on cruise control. Never mind that I had struggled—mostly unsuccessfully—to have consistent time alone with God. Forget that I had hardly spent time worshipping God offstage.

The more my wife and I searched our own souls, the more we realized we had become passive, complacent, at times even indifferent about our own knowledge of God. We had been lulled to sleep by our own apparent success, numbed into coasting by our spiritual Midas touch.

What began in the days after Thursday was a journey, a road of uncovering and discovering, of stripping away what thoughts of God we now knew were rumors and finding again the face of Christ.

These were not rumors that came from one man, one pastor. In fact, it's hard to say that any of them did. Any search for the headwaters would be misguided anyway. Because that's not the point. It's not *where* the rumors came from; it's *why* they came at all.

Here's what I've learned: Rumors grow in the absence of revelation. Every time we keep God at arm's length, declining an active, living knowledge of Him, we become vulnerable to rumors. Lulled by false comfort and half-truths about God, we—in Keith Green's famous words—fall asleep in the light.

What the Heck is Going On?

Until life comes to a screeching halt.

There are moments when time stands still. Our old vision of the world, like a scrim on a giant set, rolls up out of sight, leaving us with a jagged, stark picture of reality, its edges sharp, rough, and bare. Everything looks different, feels different. Things that once peppered our lives with meaning are now completely irrelevant and vain. Things we had ignored and overlooked are now incredibly clear, almost stunning in the forefront. The football team whose games you would never miss now seems horridly trivial. The powerful boss you were trying to impress, you now scorn and dismiss. The child you once wished would just go to sleep, you now run to hold in your arms.

A death of a loved one, the finality of divorce, the weight of debt crushing into bankruptcy—these are the moments that shake us, that wake us up and make us numb all at the same time. My moment is not that tragic in light of others. I think of a friend whose wife is facing a medically incurable disease. Or another friend whose wife decided married life was overrated and the party scene was where she belonged. I know a father who can't escape the grief of losing a child years ago. Sorrow covers him like a cape and time offers no oxygen. There is no way to compare tragic moments. The game of my-moment-is-worse-than-your-moment, while possible, is seldom profitable. Pain is acutely real to those who are breaking under its weight.

These are the "what the heck?" moments. The moments where everything stops except you, as you slowly look around. Examining. Reflecting. Puzzled. Bewildered. The silence is broken by a bellow from deep inside: "What the heck is going on?" Or some less sanitized version of the same. How could this be? And what's more, how could this be while God is with me?

The psalmists understood this feeling well. Fully two-thirds of Psalms are laments, an old-fashioned term for a "what the heck?" moment prayer. Imagine these words being prayed at church:

Why, O Lord, do you stand far off? Why do you hide yourself
in times of trouble? (Ps. 10:1)

My God, my God, why have you forsaken me? Why are you
so far from saving me, so far from the words of my groaning?
O my God, I cry out by day, but you do not answer, by night,
and am not silent. (Ps. 22:1–2)

My tears have been my food day and night, while men say to
me all day long, "Where is your God?" (Ps. 42:3)

These were covenant people, people to whom God had made an unbreakable promise, a promise to bless them, protect them, and make their days go well. So why on earth were they being pursued by enemies, losing their belongings, and getting depressed—all while watching the wicked flourish? It didn't make sense. It wasn't lining up with the covenant—or at least their understanding of it. And so they took their complaint up with God.

What's interesting is that, for the most part, we don't find out how God specifically responded. There are "psalms of Thanksgiving," where the psalmist restates his lament in the past tense—recounting how he was in trouble—and then gives thanks to God for delivering him. But the "lament psalms" grossly outnumber the "thanksgiving psalms." We don't know if all became well on earth all the time. But we are told two crucial things: the consistent character of God—good, just, faithful, loving—and the characteristic response of the psalmists—the choice to praise. In one of the psalms quoted earlier, the words of lament are followed by these words of praise:

> *Yet you are enthroned as the Holy One; you are the praise of Israel. (Ps. 22:3)*

Maybe in some ways, the Bible is written the way the Oracle in *The Matrix* prophesies: It only tells us what we need to know. It does not tell us all there is to know, only what we need for life and godliness. Here is the lesson of the psalmists: All of our experiences and emotions can become a springboard to find God and see Him for ourselves. God is present on every scene, waiting, wanting us to seek Him, believe in Him, and worship Him with every ounce of our existence.

Our discussion here is not first about suffering. The question of whether God causes it, allows it, or has nothing to do with it, has been voiced since the days in the garden. Our discussion here is simply that these moments—whether they come from our free will, the Devil's evil schemes, or God's strange providence—present us with an opportunity. Regardless of your theology, these two things are common to mankind: We all experience a measure of suffering, and every experience can be redeemed.

C. S. Lewis wrote, "God whispers to us in our pleasures, speaks in our conscience, but shouts in our pain: it is His megaphone to rouse a deaf world."[4]

Crumbs of Rumor

Too often, we walk through life with our hands fixed firmly over our eyes and ears, ignoring and avoiding the living presence of Christ with us—maybe from fear or guilt or simple apathy. But every once in awhile, our hands are pried off our faces, our eyes are almost forcibly opened, our ears are unplugged. We catch a glimpse for ourselves, a glimpse that will be our undoing. And our salvation. In that moment, we are ruined and redeemed by that little glimpse.

Job had that experience.

He never auditioned for the role, never signed up for the part. God chose him. He chose him, we are often told, to prove a point to the Devil. But I'm beginning to wonder if God chose him to show Himself to Job, to save Job from the stiff, straight lines he had drawn around God. Think about it. The story doesn't end with the Devil returning to heaven and saying, "Okay, God, You win. You were right. Job didn't curse You. He does indeed serve You for nothing in return." If that were the central tension in the story, there is a glaring lack of resolution.

A series of ridiculously unfortunate events befalls Job in a very short span of time. What takes place in the lengthy remainder of the book is a dialogue between Job, three of his friends, and a presumptuously precocious young man named Elihu. After sitting silently for seven days, the three friends can't bear to hold in their wisdom. One by one they present their cases to Job, trying to explain why he is suffering and what he should do about it. They generally agree that things have gone so poorly for Job because of some hidden sin in his life. They plead with him to go before God, repent, rid himself of his sins, and make peace with the Almighty. Job refuses. He insists on his innocence and laments to God with words that are uncomfortably honest.

Then Elihu speaks. He dismisses the elders' wisdom, preferring his own fresh insight. He is less willing to condemn Job for sin, but not as reluctant to rebuke him for pride. He hints at God's sovereignty and our inability to fully understand His ways. But he, too, echoes the familiar refrain that obedience will lead to a prosperous, pleasant life, and that disobedience will lead to tragedy and sorrow.

As arrogant and simpleminded as Job's friends may seem to us, as hard as it is to imagine ourselves saying something like that to a friend who has just lost everything, remember that they are simply articulating the prevailing wisdom of the day. It was their misguided understanding of the covenant that gave them this simple premise: Obey God, and all will be well; disobey, and you will suffer.

That formulaic and faulty view of the covenant may be the reason the book of Job is included in Hebrew Wisdom Literature. It may be that the purpose for the book of Job is to counter an overly black-and-white view of life. Perhaps God understood that humans would take the rich, profoundly unique covenant that He had made with His people and reduce it to simplistic, pithy phrases. Maybe God knows our propensity to redact the living words of relationship into rumors that spread like fire—and that sooner or later, we will get burned.

What if the book of Job is not all about some intergalactic dispute between God and the Devil? What if it's really about revelation and relationship with mortals?

At the end of the story, after Job asks God over and over with the nagging persistence of a two-year-old why he has suffered, God responds. Not with answers, but with questions—questions that bring Job to his knees. Finally Job cries:

> *I admit I once lived by rumors of you; now I have it all first-hand—from my own eyes and ears! I'm sorry—forgive me. I'll never do that again, I promise! I'll never again live on crusts of hearsay, crumbs of rumor. (Job 42:5–6 MSG)*

This is the climax of the book of Job. It's the way this incredibly moving story of suffering resolves. The mention of God restoring to Job more than what he lost is sort of an afterthought, a footnote to the story. It comes after Job finds firsthand knowledge of God. The story of Job is first and foremost a salvation story: God saved Job from small, narrow, rumor-laden views of Himself. And then Job lived holy-ever-after. It's what happens when rumors give way to revelation.

I have come to the uncomfortable realization that I have believed rumors about God that have kept me from Him, kept me from really knowing Him. I suspect I am not alone. This book is about some of the more popular rumors and the path to finding the truth. What you read here is not intended to be the basis for your view of God.

Instead, this book is an attempt to jog your mind, stir your heart, provoke your questions, and whet your appetite for the quest, for the journey that only you can take. The journey that Job took. A journey that is not necessarily one of suffering, but one that by design means eye-opening, paradigm-shattering discovery. So yes, in some sense it hurts. It's a journey that begins with your fist to the sky and can end with your knees on the earth. A journey that begins with questions and ends with speechless worship.

Mine began on a Thursday.

DISCUSSION QUESTIONS:

1. What are some of your "what the heck?" moments?

2. Do you think your knowledge of Christ is active and alive or stale and sentimental?

3. What are you looking for God to do in your heart as you read this book?

Notes

[1] Tobias Wolff, *Old School* (New York: Vintage Books, 2003), 15.

[2] Henri Nouwen, *In the Name of Jesus* (New York: Crossroad, 1989), 19–20.

[3] Henri Nouwen, *In the Name of Jesus*, 20.

[4] C. S. Lewis, *The Problem of Pain* (New York: Touchstone, 1996), 83.